# SEX, DEATH, *and* TANTRA

A MEMOIR

# ED SWAYA

Printed in the United States of America

ISBN: 978-0-578-61074-0

First Edition
10 9 8 7 6 5 4 3 2 1

*For Zachary*

# INTRODUCTION

THIS BOOK IS my story—my experience of profound loss and finding my way back to a robust life using the principles and practices of Tantra as my guide.

As I explored the application of Tantra to my healing, I was frustrated by the dearth of resources about what I was actually doing and why it might be working. Many people have preconceived ideas of Tantra and were incredulous when I spoke of using Tantra to heal from loss.

So, I set out to write about this lineage of Tantra with the hope of inspiring people to study and practice. I did not do very well at that.

I found myself telling my story—my story of love, loss, and healing. Although the details of Tantra took a back seat to my particular story, my journey is meaningless without some understanding of what Tantra is and to what principles I ascribe.

I hope those who know something about Tantra can learn about a unique application of Tantra in the service of healing from grief. For those with no previous understanding of Tantra, I hope this book serves as a jumping-off point for some conversation or exploration.

In this book I use the word 'god' to refer to something greater than my self, something transpersonal, transcendent, mysterious or mystical. God, The Divine, the gods, the goddesses, The Universe, our highest Self are other words which carry the essence of my use of the word 'god.'

# CHAPTER 1

*It is a curious thing, the death of a loved one. We all know that our time in this world is limited, and that eventually all of us will end up underneath some sheet, never to wake up. And yet it is always a surprise when it happens to someone we know. It is like walking up the stairs to your bedroom in the dark, and thinking there is one more stair than there is. Your foot falls down, through the air, and there is a sickly moment of dark surprise as you try and readjust the way you thought of things.*

—Lemony Snicket
*Horseradish: Bitter Truths You Can't Avoid*

"I'VE GOT MY keys, I've got my phone... back in forty-five minutes."

Zachary took our dog for a walk just as dusk was settling on a warm, clear summer evening.

We had just returned from a weekend at the beach with our daughter, Zoe; our friend, Nancy; and our new dog, Sophie. The weekend had been a bit magical: good wine, good food, good conversation, two dogs, and our delightful six-year-old girl. Zachary and I had taken walks, slept well, had good sex, enjoyed quiet time, laughed and—as we often did when away from home—dreamed together about our future. It was one of those close-to-perfect times families get every now and again.

Zachary did not return home from walking the dog. He was hit by a car and died three hours later. Life, as I had known it, was over.

When he did not return in an hour, I called him. No answer. I called again. I sent a text message, and then another and then another. I started to panic. I called him every two minutes.

My stomach hurt. My heart raced. After about twenty calls, someone picked up the phone. Before the woman said anything, I heard the all-too-familiar beep-beep-beep of a hospital. *Fuck!* Yes, he was there. No, he was not okay. He was in surgery. Yes, his injuries were life-threatening. He had no ID on him.

No, they could not tell me anything more.

Our Zoe was downstairs watching *ET* and Zachary had planned to watch the end of the movie with her. *Fuck. What do I do? Fuck.* I had until the end of the movie to formulate a plan.

*Hit by a car? How? What? I need to get there.* My mind was swirling. I was queasy.

I called Nancy, who lived in the neighborhood and asked her to come over and put Zoe to bed. I then called our best friend, Heather, and asked her to meet me at the hospital.

Once Nancy arrived, I took a deep breath and told my daughter one of the few lies I have told her. "I am heading out to meet Daddy at Starbucks. Nancy is here with you, and she will put you to bed."

*Just try to be normal.*

"Can I still finish the movie, Papa?" she asked.

I slightly relaxed, smiled and said, "Yes, honey. Of course... Don't forget to brush your teeth." I kissed her goodnight and went upstairs. Shaken, but breathing deeply and deliberately to keep calm, I left the house.

I was in slow motion; time began to play tricks on me. The thirty-minute trip to the hospital felt like hours. Trying to remain calm, I drove toward the hospital, slowly. Thinking about Zoe downstairs watching TV, I realized I had to be particularly careful as I drove. *Breathe.*

Three blocks from our home, police had cordoned off the main thoroughfare. I pulled over and spoke to a police officer, who told me that Zachary had not been conscious when the ambulance arrived.

He also confirmed what the voice on the phone told me: Zachary was already in surgery. *Fuck.*

The officer told me a neighbor had Sophie, but I barely registered the information.

I returned to my car and was aware that although it was a warm evening, I could not stop shivering. My chest tightened. I could hardly swallow. My teeth were chattering. I needed to drive to the hospital. There was traffic because they had closed the street—lots of traffic. *Get the fuck out of my way. I have to get to the hospital. Please.* I began to feel desperate.

When I arrived at the hospital and identified myself as Zachary's partner, I was escorted to the social worker, which I took as a very bad sign. The social worker kept saying "He's very sick... He is very sick." With each repetition of these three words, my stomach tightened just a bit more. "You should call any other family members and let them know he is here."

This made no sense to me. "I think I'll wait to see how he is before I call his family." I did not want to alarm his family unnecessarily.

The social worker gave me a sickly concerned look and said, "He is very sick... You should call family members who are close." *Those four words again. He is very sick.*

This made no sense to my brain. Zachary was a healthy, strapping, gorgeous thirty-nine-year-old man—he was my partner of fifteen years. He was not sick. He was terribly, maybe mortally, injured. Broken but certainly not sick.

I called Zachary's sister and her husband, whom she had married just three weeks before. An hour or so later they joined me in the hospital. We sat together, waiting.

After a while, a uniformed police officer approached. He officiously introduced himself and then proceeded to take out a business card with an incident number written on the front. He turned it over and began sketching out a four-lane road.

Somehow Sophie had slipped off her lead and ran into a busy street. Three of four lanes of traffic stopped, and Zachary made eye contact with one of the stopped drivers. He then followed Sophie into the street, where he was hit by a six-ty-something-year-old woman who was driving forty-three-miles-per-hour. She did not see him until she heard the thud. He slammed into her windshield at forty-three-miles-per-hour. He was thrown ninety-four feet from the point of impact.

At the accident scene, the police did a toxicology screening on her. They said they would keep me abreast of those results, but it appeared that the driver was not intoxicated and quite appropriately shaken.

When the first person arrived at Zachary's side, he found Zachary struggling to breathe.

He repositioned Zachary's body, and his breathing relaxed. When he asked Zachary if he could hear him, Zachary said, "No." That was his final word.

In the waiting room, I felt both worried and not worried. *He is very sick* made me think that the extent of his injuries was severe. But the idea that his injuries were fatal never crossed my mind in any real way.

After three long hours, we were told Zachary was finally out of surgery and on his way to the trauma ICU, where we would be able to see him. I am an excellent planner. I just knew that when I saw him, I would understand what the fuck had happened, and then I could do what I do well: plan for his most likely protracted recovery.

I was beginning to feel lost, and really wanted to see him.

Once in the ICU we, again, waited for what felt like an eternity. The waiting started to feel like another terrifying sign. A doctor finally appeared in the doorway, and he directed us into a conference room, not a patient room (yet another bad sign). There, he uncomfortably asked our relationship to Zachary. I was having trouble, and beginning to feel frightened.

I will never forget the next words he said: "I have terrible news..."

My legs physically gave out from under me. I remember dropping to my knees wondering what I was going to do. The room was spinning. Zachary's sister was screaming inconsolably, and I couldn't understand what she was saying.

"My brother!" was all I could decipher through my shock. When I remember that night, I can still hear her screams; they make my stomach hurt.

The doctor told us Zachary died in the elevator on the way from surgery to the trauma ICU. CPR was the last procedure done to his broken body. CPR—on an elevator.

My brain was stuck in a panic: *What am I going to do?*

We were finally allowed to see him. As we walked down the corridor, I felt sick. I no longer wanted to see him. I wanted to run the other way as fast as I could. I did not know how I was going to face him. *Dead.*

His body was wrecked. The doctors had not been able to stop internal bleeding from his intestines. His face was badly bruised. He had been pumped full of saline in a vain attempt to keep his blood pressure up. He looked bloated, distorted, and distended. He was intubated. His legs were broken. The doctors had not had a chance to determine how badly his brain had been damaged.

I went numb.

It was 2 AM, and I was getting antsy. I wanted to go, and I wanted to stay and never leave his body. I felt like I was splitting apart. Things were happening around me. Zachary's sister called their other siblings and then headed back to her home to wake her children to bring them back to the hospital to say goodbye to their favorite uncle. Heather's husband and twenty-year-old son arrived—the weight of the sadness in their eyes was too much for me to bear. I could not call my brother, who lived in town. I asked Zachary's sister to make that call. Finally, Nancy called from home to let me know that Zoe was fast asleep. She asked, "How is Zachary, honey?"

The lump in my throat made me hard to understand. I had to say "he died" three times before the words were intelligible.

I looked again (and again) at Zachary's bruised face and decided I would not wake Zoe to bring her to the hospital to see her dead father. I knew it was important for her to see him (his body) to say goodbye, but not like this. He was too broken. Because I was not trusting my thinking about this, I asked friends and family who were there if they thought Zoe should come that night and they all agreed it was best to leave her home and tell her in the morning.

I stared at my phone and called Ken, Zachary's and my Tantra teacher. He had helped me through emotional rough times in the past, and I knew he was someone whose presence would help keep me from falling apart. Ken arrived within the hour and sat with me, our families, and a few close friends beside Zachary's body, giving us his steady presence.

Zachary was starting to get cold. There was a small, half-inch square, part of his cheek, that felt like the man I had known and loved. The rest of him was contorted and bloated beyond familiarity. Nothing felt or looked like the Zachary who'd left home only a few hours before to walk the dog.

I did not cry. I was in shock. I kept wondering, *What am I going to do?*

Everything felt surreal—the hospital, his body, saying goodbye, who to call, intestines, blood loss, brain contusions, broken bones, black and blue, nausea, fear. It all turned into a blurry mess in my brain and body.

A few hours later, it was over. There were no more words. There was nothing left to do or say. Still in shock, there was nothing left for me to feel. I hadn't cried—I wasn't even aware yet that I hadn't cried. In this state of numbness, I thought I could drive home. Ken gently interceded and suggested that it might be better if he drove me home. As we left the hospital and walked across the street, I wondered aloud how I was going to let my six-year-old girl ever cross a street again without holding my hand? How would I protect her from a car going forty-three-miles-per-hour? How would I let her out of my sight? How would I live? How would I go on without Zachary? Ken just listened. There was nothing to say.

*Zoe. Home, sleeping in her bed. How am I going to tell our beautiful Zoe? Rather, how am I going to tell my beautiful Zoe? How am I going to tell my six-year-old that her dad was never coming home? How? How? How?*

Zachary would know what to do. He held steady and was smart in crisis mode. I often froze during these times, and never quite knew if he meant it when he said, "We'll figure it out," or "We're fine," but he always comforted me with those words. He seemed to know intuitively what to say and what a good next step was. I needed to ask him what to do now.

*He will know.*

I arrived home at 5 AM. A friend came by to bring Xanax in case I had a panic attack. I was prone to anxiety, and I knew I needed to sleep if I was to function during the next, excruciating, day. I slept about an hour before more people showed up at our house. I still hadn't cried.

My life was changing in ways I could not even imagine.

When Zoe awoke to a house full of people she immediately asked me, "Where's Daddy?"

I sat her on my lap on the overstuffed, threadbare purple chair and told her, "I have some sad news. Daddy was hit by a car and died."

"Stop teasing me," she replied.

I lost it. I cried—hard.

A lone tear ran down her cheek.

Several years later in therapy, she would recall the purple chair, the people on the couch, and feeling as if she had been kicked hard in the stomach. There was nothing I could have done to shield her from that kick-in-the-stomach pain and the ripples of pain that would continue for years after.

That day and the next days were a blur. I had to plan a funeral. I had to raise my daughter. I had to eat. I had to sleep. I had to think. I had to raise my daughter. I couldn't think. *I am afraid. A funeral? Really? Fuck. A funeral. I have to think. I am scared. I have to raise my daughter. I have to create some space for her to grieve. I have to eat. Sleep. Think. How do I plan for a funeral when I have not begun to digest the fact that he is dead? How do I plan a funeral for our friends and family without Zachary?*

My brain was not working, and I was more afraid than I had ever been.

Zachary and I had talked a lot about death. When Zoe was born, we had planned well for our deaths—at least we thought we had. Wills, powers of attorney, physician's directives, con-versations with family and friends–we'd done all these things with precision, thought, and even humor.

We had talked with Zoe a lot about death. In fact, in her six short years, she had experienced the death of my (and argu-ably her) best friend, three beloved family dogs, and one cat. With each death, we performed rituals as a family. We said to her many, many times that all things die.

"Even houses?" she asked.

"Yes, even houses die."

"Even the sky?"

"Yes, even the sky will die someday." And we always included that even we, her parents, would die. That one day even she would die.

But, who knew it would happen to us so soon? Who knew my husband would miss his fortieth birthday? I had done my Master's studies in grief and loss. I knew everything dies, but still, I could not imagine it in my life—not in my house; not to the strong, alive, physically coordinated, at-ease-in-his-body Zachary. It was just not possible.

I did not know that death sometimes comes so unexpectedly that it takes the surviving loved one's breath away.

That first day, I attended to Zoe. I had a lot of help, so my radar could be focused on her. I knew that kids often get lost when a parent is preoccupied with illness, addiction, work, death, and I was aware enough to make sure that I and friends and family paid attention to her. I could not make any calls. Others did that task for me. I rarely could answer my phone when calls came in. Ostensibly, they were calls of condolence, but they were more like "I just heard... is it true?"

These calls drained me. Friends' shock and sadness kept slamming me headlong into what was slowly becoming real.

Late in the afternoon, I made one phone call that only I could make. I called our daughter's mother, Daphne.

When she answered, she could tell something was very wrong. I assured her that Zoe was okay, but that I had some terrible news. Zachary had died. I do not think I will ever forget her agonized howl.

Daphne placed Zoe with us at birth through open adoption, a process whereby she virtually had an unlimited pool of potential adoptive parents who would gladly raise her child.

Daphne found us online (on my birthday) when she was twenty weeks along in her pregnancy. She was nineteen-years-old, and she believed the most loving thing she could do for her child would be to place her with a couple who had the time, energy, resources, and structures in place to provide the stable and loving home that she could not.

Daphne was smart, articulate, and grounded. She wanted to continue school, go to parties without the responsibility of a child. She wanted to grow into herself before she parented on her own. She also wanted to know her daughter, be in her daughter's life, and stay connected as a member of her extended family. We met Daphne a few weeks before Zoe was born.

We were at the hospital when Zoe came into the world and held her in our arms when she was only seven minutes old. Daphne, Zachary, Zoe, and I were together during those first five days before we were legally allowed to bring Zoe home.

While I knew that Daphne saw me as a solid, intelligent person who would be a good parent to her daughter, it was Zachary who charmed Daphne and connected with her in ways I could not. Daphne loved us both, but she was more emotionally connected with Zachary. He was able to make connections at times when I became socially or emotionally awkward, shy, and befuddled.

Through her tears, Daphne told me that Zachary had healed her by teaching her that families can be fun. Zachary made family fun. That was true about him. He was fun.

She honored our family—Zachary, Zoe, and me—as well as the family we created with her when she placed Zoe with us, by flying from her hometown in the Bible Belt to attend his funeral.

Somehow, I planned a funeral. He died early in the morning on a Monday, and only hours later friends were driving me to a funeral home. The sense of surreality was overwhelming. I felt separate from the people and things around me. It was the first time I'd left the house since I'd returned from the hospital at 5:00 AM. While I'd only been inside for ten hours or so, I felt like I had not seen daylight in weeks.

When I stepped outside, the light was harsh and hurt my eyes. My experience of time was distorted. I had difficulty staying in my body. I was scared to leave home. I was scared out in the world. I felt little. I felt completely vulnerable. The fear started infiltrating my body as soon as I opened the door to leave the house. Little did I know I would feel this fear for an unbearably long time.

I remember: the grass in front of the house that afternoon, the lavender, the chain-link fence, the red door; the dry, sweet, slightly dusty smell of summer, the blue car, the angle of the sun, the dark-red weeping birch tree Zachary had planted. I remember feeling disoriented.

*Breathe*, I reminded myself. Breathing is what keeps me in my body. Breathing was easy in morning meditation practice when everyone I loved was alive and safe from forty-three-mile-an-hour cars.

The spot where he was killed was on the way to the funeral home; there was no avoiding it. A roadside altar had been set up, mostly by strangers, filled with flowers, stuffed animals, and notes. My friends and I stopped and stood there, silent, stunned, awkwardly looking at notes of condolence from people we did not know. It was not believable that this altar was connected to me in any way. The whole experience continued to be surreal. *The blacktop, marked with orange spray-painted arrows, circles, dotted lines, trajectories, and a symbol—an orange circle with an "X" in the center, on his final landing spot some ninety-four feet from where he was hit.*

My stomach hurt. I had to remind myself to breathe repeatedly. My stomach was churning, my breath was labored, I was light-headed.

We drove to the funeral home and parked. As I crossed the street, I became aware that a part of me was overwhelmed with a sickening combination of horror, dread, fear, and disbelief. I crossed streets all the time. I was crossing one at that moment. *How was it that my husband was hit by a car and is now dead? And how is it that I am going to talk about a funeral? More immediately, how am I going to cross a busy street?*

I had watched enough of the HBO series *Six Feet Under* to know what to expect. The funeral home was very appropriately subdued, but I was expected to make decision after decision about location, casket, flowers, clothes, numbers, venue. I wanted to be sick. Who knew one could rent a casket? I did not really believe it was happening to me, to my life. Despite my body's unequivocal visceral response, I was in denial that this was real. Sometimes our minds are slow to grasp what is plain and simply true. Sometimes it takes years.

When we had planned for our deaths, Zachary made it clear that he did not want to be embalmed or have his body viewed. But even in the hospital, after I decided not to wake Zoe so she could see Zachary's body that night, I knew that I wanted her to have the option to view his body. Unless I see a body, I do not believe someone is actually dead, and I did not want to misstep any part of the grieving process for Zoe. My best guess was that seeing her dad's body would help Zoe grieve.

He was to be embalmed and prepared for viewing. *Sorry, Zachary, I am blatantly not doing as you wished.*

I'm still not sure that was the best decision. His wishes conflicted with what I thought was best for Zoe. I was in no shape to get the embalmers good photos of Zachary and left that to friends who did not have great pictures. He looked nothing like himself when he was in his casket. *Nothing.*

Logistics—we talked about people, ritual, location, and time. People were coming in from out of town. We selected Thursday as the day for the funeral. It would have been the ninth anniversary of our wedding. *Our ninth wedding anniversary? Can I bear this pain?* I asked the friend who'd officiated at our wedding ceremony to officiate at the funeral.

Jim was smart, a gifted orator and a dear friend. More than 250 people from all parts of our life came to celebrate Zachary's life and to mark the beginning of life without him. Jim eulogized him well, touching on Zachary's love of animals, his love of me and Zoe, his career path, his family, and his character. I do not remember much of what he said during his eulogy, but I do remember people coming up to speak about their unique relationship with Zachary. I asked our friend Susan, who is also a therapist, to be Zoe's person at the funeral, as I knew I would be deep in my own grief.

At the funeral, Zachary's sister spoke about her love of her brother and of his generosity with her kids. While she spoke, Zoe went to the podium and stood with her—bitter/sweet. Teachers from the school where Zachary worked as a first-grade teacher spoke about the lightness and humor he had brought to the staff. Parents of his students spoke about his uncanny ability to connect with their particular and peculiar kids; friends spoke about wine and humor, and neighbors spoke about his ability to use a jackhammer and bake killer blackberry pies. I did not speak. I could not speak.

Planning a funeral was not my only logistical challenge. Zachary, Zoe, and I had moved to the city two years earlier after living in a small town for thirteen years. We'd loved the rural lifestyle: not owning a house key, leaving our keys and wallets in the car so we wouldn't lose them, and running into friends at the Saturday farmer's market, discussing important matters like worm bins and chainsaws. We knew we wanted to spend the rest of our life there. So we sold our house and bought a magical forested piece of land on a lake nearby, where we planned to build our dream home. In the meantime, Zachary wanted to live in the city for a change of pace. I reluctantly agreed. Because I worked in the city, I thought I'd go crazy not getting away to the quiet of the country at the end of the day. But it turned out that we all loved living in the city.

Gone for me were the days of long commutes and traffic. I walked twenty minutes to work each day, enjoying urban gardens along the way and saying 'hi' to neighbors and their dogs. We delighted in new restaurants, theater, and nightlife. It was a fun adventure before our next stage of life in the country could start.

The week we were to break ground on our new house, Zachary was killed. While I was able to avoid many of the calls from friends and family that week, I could not avoid talking with the contractors, bankers, and county officials to put the dream house project on hold. I choked on these words.

From the moment Zachary died, I knew that I did not want this tragedy to be the moment Zoe remembered as the instant her life went to shit. I hoped that this would be a time she remembered as immensely challenging and even crappy, but not a time when her life went irretrievably sideways. My main focus as we went through the rituals surrounding Zachary's death was my commitment to helping Zoe create a good life from this rubble. *But how am I going to do that?*

Everyone offered to help. I was lost. I did not know what to ask for, or how to figure out what I needed. *How can I know what it is that I want or need when my heart is broken? When my stomach feels like it has just been kicked?* The energy in my body was choppy and disconnected. My stomachache seemed to be at odds with my heartache, but my brain needed energy flowing well between all body parts to make the right decisions. I was hardly eating and hardly pooping. Things were just not flowing.

*If only I could just think…*

It was hard to breathe, no less think… and I needed to think.

# CHAPTER 2

*Sex is a part of nature. I go along with nature.*

—*Marilyn Monroe*

NEITHER ZACHARY NOR I was involved with organized religion, so when he died, I didn't have the comfort of believing he was in heaven or had "gone home" in any way. The truth was, I had no idea where he went after he died. It was a terribly lost feeling. Where was he?

I grew up in a low-key Orthodox Christian home complete with a stint as an altar boy and a good dose of Sunday School. Yet, as I grew older, I was no longer comfortable identifying as Christian.

A decade before I met Zachary, I'd started looking for a meaningful spiritual practice that would help me connect to the great Mysteries of Life—or whatever you want to call it.

I first heard about Tantra when I was in my early twenties from my spiritual mentor. He told me, in no uncertain terms, that I was to study Tantra. I found books about it, and at first blush, the idea of sacred sexuality excited me. I liked the concept of the marriage of sex and spirit, including orgasms that bring whole-body pleasure, a connection to God, and documented health benefits. I am not clear why, but the ideas resonated with me. I wanted to experience those things.

But every time I tried to get through a book about Tantra, I was derailed after about fifteen minutes. The authors all described Tantra as a path to God that was expressed through the erotic connection or spiritual/sexual marriage between a man and a woman. I could not find a place for me, a gay man, to access this spiritual tradition. Gay sex seemed not to exist in Tantra.

I was frustrated because I wanted to use my powerful erotic desires and behaviors to... to... to do *something*. I couldn't articulate it, but I felt in my gut that Tantra was the pathway to something greater than myself. I wanted to connect my eroticism and sexuality with my still-not-quite-defined spiritual practices. While sacred sexuality made sense to me, the path remained elusive to me as a gay man.

Throughout our relationship, whenever I shared my feelings of longing to explore Tantra with Zachary, he made light of the idea. He loved sex, but he thought that the marriage of sex and spirit was a joke: perfect fodder for innuendo and eye rolling. While he loved me and sensed my earnestness, he was not at all interested in this exploration. Or so I thought. Or so he said—at least not then.

Twenty years after my interest in Tantra had been sparked, I reconnected with one of my counseling mentors. Ken had led the consultation group for therapist interns at an agency where I was an intern, and I'd had a huge crush on him those many years ago. He was boyishly cute, brilliant, experienced, and a natural teacher. When I first became a therapist, he and I tried to organize an outdoor therapy adventure for men, but not enough participants signed up. Later, he was the clinical

ED SWAYA

director of a research project at the local university, and I was on the team of therapists. We superficially kept in touch and had lunch once a year or so.

Then Ken began referring his "sacred intimate" clients to me for traditional psychotherapy, although at the time I didn't understand what a "sacred intimate" was.

Over time, our now-shared clients began to speak of what sounded to me like highly erotic counseling work they were doing with Ken. One day over lunch, Ken explained that he used the principles of Tantra in his role as a sacred intimate. He did traditional psychotherapy in one office, and across town, he did erotic healing work in another space. I was intrigued by the idea of using sex to heal with Tantra as the foundation but summarily dismissed the idea that he could be a teacher for me. That was a boundary I wasn't prepared to cross. As my practice with the clients he was referring progressed, I witnessed the power of combining traditional psychotherapy and sacred sexual healing work. Over time, I became increasingly intrigued.

During one of our now weekly lunches, I started to understand Ken's explanation of "sacred intimate" work. That night I talked with Zachary about sacred sexuality in the service of emotional healing, but he still did not seem interested.

"It's amazing... Ken was actually fucking someone and having what sounds like a therapeutic conversation with him," I told him. "While inside of this guy, they were talking about why this client feels 'bored' while he gets fucked.

"Imagine," I said, my mind racing, "what kind of information shows up when you do something like counseling while inside of someone?" I was jumping out of my skin thinking of the possibilities.

"Uh-huh, I bet I could do that too." Zachary grinned while making a gesture like he was fucking someone. We both laughed.

Zachary used to laugh with me about psychotherapy in general, saying he could never "listen to people whine" all day for his work. He knew he would be a terrible psychotherapist.

"However," he said with feigned interest, "maybe I could be a sexual intimate... is that what Ken calls it?"

Several times I clumsily tried to introduce more "conscious sexuality" into our relationship, while really having no idea what "conscious sexuality" actually was. I tried to slow down while we were playing; I tried to breathe together while we were inside of one another; I tried to stop and talk (I am a therapist after all) in the middle of our sexual play; I tried to maintain eye contact for longer and longer periods of time— and was frustrated with the wall I hit each and every time. I felt derailed, not even sure I was correctly practicing "conscious sexuality."

We were having highly fun and intense sex pretty regularly, and Zachary was not interested in fixing what was clearly not broken. But despite our very sexually alive and adventurous relationship, I wanted something more from him. *From us. For us.*

Then I received an unexpected e-mail from Ken. He and his partner of twenty-five-years were having a party. While I had known Ken professionally for almost that long, we had never socialized. There was a small footnote on the bottom of the invitation saying something along the lines of, "If you are getting this e-mail and we have not seen much of you recently, please know that in some way you have been important in our lives." It was that footnote that made it possible for me to consider the invitation. I briefly considered going.

Because of Zachary's prurient interest in Ken and his work, I forwarded the e-mail to him, mostly for a laugh. Even though I was deeply interested in the practice and he was not, we always had an easy time laughing about our differences. Surprisingly, he wrote back, "Let's go!"

He wanted to go. *He wanted to go? Huh?*

I did not want to go. I did not know Ken outside of an occasional lunch over the years. I was beginning to get to know Ken over our more frequent lunches now that we shared clients. I did not know Ken's partner or kids. I did not know Ken's friends or community. I was shy. I like the idea of new social situations, but I am often uncomfortable entering them. In fact, I dread them.

We went.

Zachary and Ken hit it off. Zachary was charming and charmed Ken.

Ken was charming and charmed Zachary. I was shy and awkward. There was some sweet flirting and playful conversation between the two of them about Ken's work. Zachary's curiosity was piqued, and Ken invited us to continue our fragmented cocktail conversation at another time. We agreed to meet up and talk more.

A week later, Zachary and I met Ken at a nondescript leather-ish gay bar. We had a beer and Zachary jumped right in and asked about Tantra. The questions were simple: "What is it?" How are sex and spirituality related? What precisely is sexual energy?"

Ken told us about his ten years of study with his teacher. "My teacher lived in India for thirty years and had never taught Tantra in the West until he met me. We did a ton of experiments—many, but certainly not all, were erotic—to figure out ways for me to learn. He learned Tantra through meditation, cooking, and surprisingly little eroticism when he lived in India."

*Cooking? Really?*

"He is a trusted mentor; intimate friend; occasional yet intimate lover; and a wise, nonjudgmental counselor for me," Ken said of his Tantra teacher. "We absolutely love one another."

Their relationship was not based on what I would normally think of as sexual desire, but more on respect and desire to learn and explore together. *A sexual relationship not based on sexual attraction?* Tantra sounded far different from what I had imagined.

From what Ken was describing, sex was the tool or arena for self-exploration. None of the experiences with his teacher were about who put what where and how. Yet there seemed to be a lot of sexual and erotic play. Although dots were connecting, the picture remained elusive.

"I never understood my strong, almost compulsive, desire to have sex," Ken said. "But in both Tantra and psychotherapy, we know that compulsion is often just a shade away from spiritual yearning."

*Right. I know this.*

In Alcoholics Anonymous, the problem of alcohol consumption is considered a spiritual one. Other compulsive behaviors I see in my practice are always linked to a yearning for something more significant, with more meaning, broader than self—transcendent.

I was losing myself in thoughts about sex, healing, God, the Sacred, etc., when I was distracted by the sound of laughter and playful banter. Zachary had that look he always had when he was flirting. I looked at Ken's boyish face and body that I'd been so enamored of some twenty-five-years earlier.

I appreciated his warm eyes and the gentle weathering of his face. My attraction to him was still there. I felt some warmth that surprised me.

Just as Zachary was asking Ken more questions about Tantra and sexual energy, I had to step away to pee. My mind was racing, connecting fragments of information I had gleaned over the last twenty years. *Sex, healing, pleasure, shame, God... cooking?*

When I came back, I found Zachary and Ken making out—seriously making out. I stopped dead in my tracks and watched, indulging my voyeurism without disturbing what was happening. It was hot. I noticed that a handful of men in the bar were also watching and they seemed to be getting turned on by Zachary and Ken's sexual energy. I could feel that energy quite palpably in my gut and beginning erection. From the way their bodies intertwined, Ken and Zachary were most certainly feeling it too.

I became shy (as I often do in new sexual situations), yet tentatively joined them. Now the three of us were making out. We made out some more. The three of us, mouths to mouths, tongues dancing, sharing saliva and breath. *Three men sharing breath, breathing in one another's essences and mixing in our own as we exhaled. It felt intoxicating. Sharing breath? What is going on?*

Interspersed with our kissing and our shared breathing, we took breaks to talk about Tantra and life. We then made out some more and talked some more. We took turns breathing into one another's mouths. While Zachary and I would steal an afternoon here and there to fuck and talk all day, it was most certainly not my habit to engage in eroticism and stop in the middle of a sexually charged moment to have a meaningful conversation and then go back to having sex. What the three of us were doing was different, and interesting. I was slightly aware of the energy building up and moving around in my body.

While we made out, the other men in our area of the bar were peripherally engaged in our play. Some talked with us, some watched, some were even curious about our conversation.

Zachary insisted that he needed to be convinced that there was such a thing as sacred sexuality when he knew that being convinced was not really possible. He used his skepticism to flirt with Ken, and Ken responded to Zachary's flirtations with increasingly refined explanations about Tantric philosophy (which made me as hard as the making out did), as well as an increased physical intensity.

The specifics about Tantra that Ken was explaining were jumbled in my mind as we continued our high-intensity, fully clothed, three-way make-out. I was mixing my fledgling intellectual understanding about Tantra (which is compelling for me) with the sexual energy of making out. I needed to stop. I needed time to breathe and integrate. I needed time to make sense of what was happening.

What I started to learn from Ken that first day, and what I continue to discover, is that Tantra does not offer neat and tidy narratives as many spiritual traditions do. Tantra opens doors that open more doors, and these pathways are pleasurable, complex, challenging, and very sexy.

We talked and made out for a couple of hours. After a couple more beers, we called it a night.

When Ken left, Zachary and I felt as though we were high. Neither of us could really explain it, but our minds and bodies were decidedly altered. We'd only made out and talked, yet we both felt sexually satisfied—as though we had cum. While the feeling was curious for me, it was a bit shocking for Zachary. We'd had enough fun, random sex during our fourteen years together to know that something out of the ordinary had just happened. We did not have any idea what it was, and we knew we wanted to learn more.

Over the next few days, Zachary and I, together and separately, mulled over our experience. He grew more skeptical; I grew more intrigued. He chalked up our good feelings to high-intensity flirting and interesting conversation. He denied that there was anything remotely spiritual about it. But while he was skeptical, Zachary was a consummate adventurer and was curious to do more. There was rarely a sexual adventure to which Zachary said "no."

During our bar make out session, when Zachary challenged Ken about using sex to heal and/or to deepen one's spirituality, Ken repeatedly invited Zachary to have "a session" with him.

"Tantra can only be talked about for so long... to understand Tantra, it must be learned by heart, in your body... Come. You can learn by doing."

By the end of that night, I knew that I would soon have sessions with Ken to learn Tantra. And I had a suspicion that Zachary would also want to try a session or two. It was just out there enough, sexy enough, and interesting enough for Zachary to want to experience this. So we talked it over with Ken, and Zachary decided to have a sacred sexuality healing session with Ken.

When I speak of my relationship with Zachary, I say (and mean it) that we were monogamous. I know that this categorization is by all linguistic and behavioral standards inaccurate. However, for me (and for him) it was true. We had agreed that all of our sexual energy was to be shared and experienced together. We were both very erotic and sexual beings and enjoyed having sexual experiences with other men. However, we wanted to have some sort of container or structure that held our sexuality sacred and was only shared by us.

We agreed that we would engage in sex with other men only when we both desired such an activity, and when we were both present and engaged. This "container" worked well for us.

I was an out-of-the-closet gay counselor working fairly publicly in the gay community and Zachary was a first-grade teacher. Because we were both somewhat visible, we decided that we would not engage in sexual encounters in or around our town. We agreed that it would add unwanted and unnecessary drama and complexity to our lives if we ended up in erotic/sexual spaces with clients or parents. We established agreements about specific behaviors (for example, we never got fucked by strangers—that was ours) and about sexual safety. We did not engage sexually with men we knew, and we did not have ongoing sexual relationships with other men.

So our "container" consisted of shared desire, being emotionally and physically present, not sharing certain sexual practices with others, and only including others when we were out of town. It was brilliant! This container allowed us to have explorations, pleasures, learning, experiences, and down-and-dirty fun, while still holding our hearts and souls. It was this container that held our hearts bonded together in our "monogamous" relationship.

As Zachary, Ken, and I talked about Zachary's upcoming session, I grew uncomfortable. How would it fit into our container? Zachary no doubt was going to engage erotically with Ken, who lived and worked in our city and was someone who we knew. They would likely develop an ongoing relationship. Zachary and I talked a lot about this. It was uncomfortable for us as we had conflicting desires: we wanted to learn Tantra, we wanted to learn Tantra with Ken as our teacher, and we wanted to trust the relationship container that had supported us so well this last decade. Ken told Zachary and me, "You don't find Tantra; Tantra finds you." Now it seemed to have found us and was about to both disturb and expand our container.

After much wrangling, we decided that it would be valuable for both of us if I were in the room as an observer during Zachary's session. Being there honored a key component of our container—to be present with each other when engaging with others sexually. We talked with Ken about this, and while he had never done a session with an observer (and a partner observer, no less), Ken thought it would work well.

"Remember, there are no good or bad experiments," Ken said, as we talked with him about our conflicting desires. "I will always encourage you to follow your desires, but the trick is to know yourself well enough to know what desires are more meaningful for you.

"Meditate. Talk. Feel. And at some point, you will realize Tantric sessions are experiments where everyone learns something. It is not that big of a deal."

*It's not that big of a deal?*

I kept thinking that making the right decision was essential as if something like the "right" decision exists.

The three of us were up for this experiment.

We arrived at Ken's studio at the appointed hour, and I was nervous. Zachary, dressed in his well–planned, super-casual jeans and T-shirt, was excited. His eager, adventurous spirit was comforting and endearing to me. Not so secretly, I was also a bit envious of it; I wished I did not lead with anxiety when I approached new situations.

We set up Ken's studio space so that they were sitting on a futon couch toward the center.

I was apart from them, but still very much present for them and myself. I could easily and comfortably see and hear them, and they me, so I felt like I was included in their session although I was not physically engaged with them. I saw my role as "holding space" for what was to unfold, bringing loving presence to the moment. I was not there to mold or shape or even influence what was about to happen; instead, I was there to bear witness with an open heart and mind. I felt that I became part of the woven tapestry of their experience, and I was participating in a subtle, energetic way.

We began with a ten-minute unguided meditation to allow each of us to ground and be present in our bodies, and perhaps clearer about our own thoughts, assumptions, and expectations.

As we gently came out of our meditation, the session palpably shifted when Ken asked Zachary, "What would you like right now?"

This seemingly simple question challenged Zachary's life-long perception of himself as a man.

My husband was model gorgeous. He had a traditionally enviable (perfect, to me) lean, well-defined, well-proportioned, six-foot, two-inch body, with handsome German features, smooth skin, and a winning smile—and he was charming to boot. While he had a myriad of physical, social, sexual, emotional, and practical skills, he relied on his looks as an entrée into unfamiliar worlds. People (men, women, gay, straight, kids, grown-ups) all wanted to be close to Zachary. His self-perception was skewed—it tricked him into thinking their desire for connection or closeness to him was because he was handsome. He would not or could not see that people wanted to be close with him for his heart and mind.

Unlike me, he was comfortable with being approached. In erotic situations, he was comfortable with being desired. He would show up, and sexual buzz would happen around him. Zachary was often the star, and he had much from which to choose. His erotic choices overwhelmed him with delightful options. He was happy responding to the desires of others. He was not accustomed to thinking about his own desires. Instead, his habit was to respond graciously to what was offered to him.

When Ken gently asked, "What do you want?" I noticed Zachary's relaxed body tighten up just a bit and his smile subtly contort. He was anxious. Zachary and I both had assumed that this spiritual healing session would involve Ken presenting him with something Tantric (whatever that meant) to do. Zachary didn't expect to be asked about his desire. This unexpected interruption of his habit to respond to the sexual advances allowed for something new to emerge.

Ken was spot-on with this intervention. My mind was swirling with delight.

Perhaps it was mildly sadistic, but I was excited to see Zachary's discomfort. I knew he struggled with owning desires. And I knew he would be more authentically himself if he allowed himself to embrace his desires. *How did Ken know this? How did he get here so fast with Zachary?*

As much as this did not look like a Tantric offering, it most certainly was. A cornerstone practice of Tantra is noticing and trusting your desire. This sounds easy and fun, but sometimes it is neither. To trust your desire, you have to know your body, mind, and spirit.

Zachary's first erotic healing session began the process of my understanding that knowing your body and mind is the heart and soul of Tantra.

In our Western Judeo-Christian society, trusting desire is a radical notion. Before beginning my Tantric practice, I cannot recall a moment in my life when I was given implicit or explicit permission to trust that my desire was good, healthy, and might even lead me closer to God. Rather, I can remember many instances where I was taught to be suspicious of my desire and my pleasure. I internalized the message that I shouldn't trust desire. Pleasure and desire were secretive, suspect, furtive, and best left unspoken. Trusting desire is a practice cultivated in the study of Tantra; as the practice deepens, the practitioners discern deeper desires and pleasures.

Zachary finally responded to Ken's question. He asked Ken to hold him. Ken wrapped his arms around Zachary and held him. At first, Zachary's body was tense, and then slowly began to relax. Zachary's arms and legs let go of some of the tension they were holding. His face softened.

After a few minutes, Ken asked, "Are you getting what you want?" Zachary said that he was.

Ken asked him if there were any more desires he had for their time together.

"Just hold me some more," Zachary said.

Again, after a few minutes, Ken asked, "Are you getting what you want?"

Zachary said he wanted them to take their shirts off. Ken held him, skin against skin. A few minutes later, Zachary asked if they could kiss. They did. The kiss began slowly and then gradually got more intense and urgent.

Ken gently pulled away and asked, "Are you getting what you want?"

Every few minutes, when it seemed as Ken and Zachary were getting lost in pleasure, Ken would stop and asked him two questions: "Are you getting what you want?" and "What do you want now?" Each time, Zachary struggled to know what he wanted and how to ask for it.

"Can we get naked?"

"Can you suck my cock?"

"Can you continue sucking?"

"May I suck your cock?"

With each pause, Ken told Zachary to breathe deeply; this would allow him to get more information about his desire. Breath, intention, sex, stillness, movement—all happening both subtly and overtly. I took Ken's cue and focused on my breathing.

It was clear to me, holding the space, that both of them were deeply enjoying their exploration of each other's bodies. Each time Ken (with a hard-on and an openness in his eyes) stopped to ask questions, I could see that he was putting seemingly unnatural pauses in their engagement. Zachary had to stay conscious of his desire and connected to his body in a different way than he usually did during sex. They were conscious and intentional in their engagement with their desires.

Zachary was being initiated into a fundamental Tantric practice: consciousness around sexuality. How often in a sexual adventure does one stop and check-in to actually feel if one is getting what one wants? I rarely did. The conscious pursuit of desire (and consciously experiencing the results of said pursuit) is at the root of Tantric practice. Conversely, the unconscious pursuit of desire is often addiction.

Watching the session, I also experienced pleasure. But my pleasure was less body-centered and more heart-and mind-centered than my husband's. At that moment, I loved him for his courage to engage erotically in a way that was completely unfamiliar and unintuitive to him. My heart was wide open for him. I was also excited because I had an inkling of the power he and Ken were accessing by being conscious during sexual play.

I felt a swirl of ideas and energies and feelings shift something inside. I was both turned on and excited intellectually by the idea of conscious sexual play. *What do I want? Am I getting what I want? Where is my pleasure? What is my desire?*

Snippets from our bar conversation with Ken echoed in my mind. *Sex heals. Deep pleasures invite deep healing. No shame in desire. Everything is an experiment.* As I watched Zachary and Ken sharing pleasure with each other, I looked at what they were doing as a series of fun experiments where they stopped every so often to gather data.

*Experiments? Data collection? Seems simple enough.*

It was sexy, and so much more than just hot sex. It was bigger than that—more expansive, full of potential for... something. I wasn't totally clear yet on what that something was, but I wanted to find out.

When Zachary and I first began our study of Tantra, I wanted the four-hour orgasm that Sting refers to when he publicly shares his experiences about Tantra. In my naiveté,

I thought all I had to do was learn a few moves here and a few breaths there and, *ta da!*—I too would enjoy four-hour orgasms.

Not so—I had to get my life torn from me, my gut kicked in, and my heart broken open before I was to have orgasms unlike any I had previously experienced. And, sorry to say, they do not (yet) last four hours.

# CHAPTER 3

*Eros guides us to Logos.*

—*Plato*

WEEKS AFTER ZACHARY and Ken's session, Ken and his colleague were leading a weekend workshop for new students in the principles and practices of Tantra. Zachary and I discussed it and decided we wanted to participate. We were excited about continuing our Tantric journey.

Even though it would take place in the city where we lived (which meant changing our monogamy container to include erotic engagement with people we might run into during our daily lives) we decided to sign up.

Of course, there were complications. Two of my psychotherapy clients had partners who were attending the same workshop. I would never knowingly engage erotically with anyone related to any of my psychotherapy clients. As a counselor, I have a duty to protect the integrity of the counseling relationship, and knowingly entering erotic space with the intimate partners of clients is not good clinical practice. This workshop was going to be taught by the only Tantra teacher of whom I knew of for gay men in the United States.

I was conflicted. I meditated a bunch. Zachary and I talked extensively. Ken, Zachary, and I talked extensively. I wanted to trust my desire to explore Tantra. I wanted to figure out how to handle changes to Zachary's and my time-tested relationship container.

In the end, we decided to go.

I also needed to be both clear and transparent with my clients about my intentions. I spoke with each one individually to let them know as much as I knew about my participation in this upcoming workshop. I really had no idea what to expect, so I could not offer them a lot of useful information about what their partners' and my time would be like together.

I decided I would not engage erotically with the participants with whom I had a psychotherapy connection. This stipulation was awkward logistically, but doable, and made sense to my clients and their partners. While Ken was fully supportive of my decision, he encouraged me to let go of being a therapist in this setting.

The entire situation made me a bit nervous. In addition to issues concerning my practice, sorting out how to honor strong competing desires while honoring our time-tested relationship container was complicated. Here, I was going to be initiated into a fundamental practice of Tantra. *How to sort out surface desires from deeper ones? How to go for deep desires thoughtfully and with care?* Trusting desire sounds easy, but it is complicated and calls for knowing one's self well.

Zachary was less conflicted about his and our participation. He was excited and eager.

WE ARRIVED AT the Tantra temple, a nondescript building in a residential area of town, on Friday after dinner. I was nervous. There were twelve participants from all walks of life. As the time to begin approached, people were milling about the main meeting space chatting about their careers, their homes, their dogs, and how they ended up here this weekend. I made it a point to introduce myself to the partners of my clients to share some small talk with them and acknowledge our complicated connection. Each of the men had been in therapy before, had attended erotic workshops, and seemed quite at ease with our connection. Once again, my anxiety about them ended up being anxiety about me.

Like a typical workshop, there were introductions and getting-to-know-you exercises. But unlike the dozens of personal growth and spiritual workshops I've attended over the years, these getting-to-know-you exercises ended up with all twelve of us standing in a circle naked—and smiling.

*Relief.*

This was an excellent beginning to a workshop!

The exercises started slowly, with gentle eye gazing and easy touching. Over the course of an hour or two, with much laughter (and nervous sweat), we moved into more challenging exercises. In one exercise, we were coached on how to say "No." Clearly, when working or playing with others erotically, being able to say "no" to any given request or exercise is vital.

In one early exercise, the instructors asked us to ask our randomly assigned partners to hand over their debit cards with PINs for the weekend—laughter. This exercise was an easy one to practice—just say "No." I complied.

I then asked the sexy thirty-something-year-old man across from me, "May I have your debit card and PIN for the weekend?"

He walked over to his bag, fished out his wallet, and looked me directly in the eye.

"Here, the PIN is 5645."

I hesitated, became flustered, and took the card. It was so unexpected that we both laughed, but his gift of trust was necessary for me when later in the workshop, I lost my shit and was in quite the puddle of tears.

One exercise profoundly changed my erotic life. We were instructed to ask our partners to do something to us for our pleasure for three minutes while we were both fully clothed. My partner, Max, was a year younger with a handsome face, winning smile, sexy body, and a full head of thick, dark hair. I asked him for something benign and unmemorable.

When it was his turn, he looked me directly in the eye. "I want you to pull my hair. I want you to pull my hair, hard. Really. Don't be shy."

The look on my face must have betrayed my reticence.

"Don't be afraid. It will be fun. I want to feel your strength." He assured me while flashing a calming, toothy smile.

I pulled Max's hair. As I pulled (firmly at first) his cheek fell into my chest, and his knees buckled. I was immediately turned on—a lot! I was surprised at my reaction. Completely in charge, I was pulling his hair, reading and responding to his body's responses and desires. I was dominating, and he was submitting. I was administering pain-consciously and thoughtfully. He was asking to receive this pain or sensation.

The energy exchange was palpable. My head spun with delight. I was surprised to notice the discomfort of my erection straining against my pants. The deeper he went into his pleasure at my hands, the deeper I went into mine. The more turned on I became, the deeper his pleasure response. The harder I pulled, the more he wanted. The harder I pulled, the more erotically charged I felt. This experience is what the masters mean when they talk about power exchange— the marriage of yin and yang. The intensity happened in all of three minutes but has taken me years to unpack and integrate into my sense of self.

At the end of that first evening, we were a group of twelve naked men standing in a circle looking at one another's eyes and bodies.

During the ride home that night, and in bed later, Zachary and I talked and talked and laughed about our experiences. We went to bed feeling closer to each other than when we'd awakened that morning—a very sweet moment.

The next day, our group discussed the importance of conscious erotic play in Tantra. The instructors explained that erotic energy is the fuel and juice that we run on as humans. In our lineage, erotic play generates our life force. We use sexy/sexual erotic energy all the time—while working, gardening, or fucking. Hearing that eroticism is something to treasure and nurture, I was struck by how different this is to my previous spiritual experiences. In Sunday school, church, and at home, eroticism was a deliberate omission.

I am not clear why, but I'd always believed that erotic play was somehow sinful, wrong, shameful, and to be avoided. The weave of God, sex, and family expectations were at odds with my religious, family and cultural upbringing.

Yet here I was sitting with a dozen men framing eroticism and sexual play as holy and necessary and good. We were not fucking and sucking; we were trying to digest the idea that the energy that most gay men have been told was an abomination might actually be sacred. Our inborn erotic energy might actually be the path to God; necessary to embrace in order to live a more whole and ethical life. Sexual energy was not to be avoided but celebrated. Tantra was a tradition thousands of years old with play and eroticism at its center.

We broke into groups of three or four to practice generating erotic energy with intention.

Gay men in various stages of undress are pretty good at getting sexy and sexual. However, we are not that practiced in getting sexy and sexual with intention and consciousness. This was our task. We were asked to practice becoming comfortable with asking for and receiving pleasure, and then "simply" holding that energy in our bodies in whatever way that made sense to each of us.

My mind was racing. *Specifically ask for what I want from another for my pleasure? Is it okay to ask for that? Is it okay to want that at all? What if what I ask is not sexy to him? What if I'm not sexy to him? What if what if what if?* As what often happens with me, my head got in the way of asking for what I wanted. Once again the simple question, "What do I want?" was deeply challenging.

I kept hearing Ken's voice. "There's no right or wrong desire, everything is an experiment. Regardless of what you ask for or are too shy to ask for, realize that your request is just an experiment. And with every experiment, don't forget to gather the data."

After each of these awkward and sometimes sexy groupings, we were asked to stop and "gather the data" from the experiments we had just performed.

"Remember, everything is an experiment," Ken reminded us. "When you asked for pleasure, did you get what you wanted? Did you ask for what you really wanted?"

*I've heard these questions before... They are questions designed to deepen our awareness of our erotic and psychological selves. Simple questions. Challenging answers.*

Some of the smaller groups I was in that day were sexier than others. Energies of the individual men together made the groups work or sometimes not work for me. Being in groups with men to whom I was not attracted was surprisingly challenging. For the final exercise of the day, I found myself mentally jumping ahead of the group and 'figuring out' the configuration of my next 'random' group. Feeling particularly smart that I had cracked the code, I manipulated the entire group so that I would be with certain men and not others.

*Success! Relief.*

Just as I was relaxing into the group that I had formed, I realized one of the men in the group was one with whom I was not going to engage erotically. At that point, we all realized our shuffle was not quite complete. As my mind raced to keep myself with men who I wanted to be with (men I found sexually attractive) Zachary quickly stepped in and switched places with me, landing me in the very group that I had tried so hard to avoid.

*Fuck.*

My stomach hurt with anxiety and disappointment— I was suddenly deeply embarrassed about my manipulation. My face flushed with shame. I had tried to take care of myself "through manipulation," as Ken would remind me when we debriefed, and my effort had backfired.

I was precisely where I did not want to be. I had struggled all day accessing my sexy erotic energy with some of these men. At times I literally and figuratively was not able to get it up.

The gist of this last small group activity was to take turns asking for some sort of erotic attention from the other three men. The previous night when the whole group had engaged in the ritual of undressing, I'd been placed with these same three men. The intention of that ritual had been to undress one another with love and care and some sexiness.

Even though I was not particularly attracted to these men, I felt I had been able to access some erotic energy, my erotic energy, while I was assisting them with their undress. However, I hadn't sensed any eroticism from them toward themselves or to any of the others in our group of four. I felt a bit awkward and not at all sexy. There was a reason I had been trying to avoid these particular men for what was going to be a longer erotic exercise.

At the end of the first night, after the rather flat undressing ritual, I privately asked Ken what to do in a situation when you either do not feel erotic energy from or toward the person with whom you are paired.

"Tantra is about being able to access your own erotic energy 24/7 regardless of where you are or what you're doing. You practice generating erotic energy in different situations so you can later have the freedom and ability to access this energy whenever you want it. Remember, Tantra is about freedom, and if you need someone to be a specific kind of sexy for you to access your erotic energies, you are limited and less free."

What he was saying was helping me to understand something that I'd been missing—engaging erotically with others even when I didn't find them sexy is the practice. Erotic energy comes from within, not from the other person. I don't think this is how most men operate, at least not in my experience.

We feel turned on, and we attribute that turned on-ness to the external stimulation of someone or something hot.

Ken's words echoed in my mind: "Your job is to find a way into your own erotic energy and learn how to nurture that rather than hoping and searching for someone else to turn you on."

*Right, freedom.*

Keeping Ken's words in mind, I stood there trying to bring my erotic self to the small group of men with whom I felt no erotic connection. It was a disaster.

As much as I wanted to follow Ken's advice and generate my own erotic energy, I couldn't. Instead, I fell back on old patterns of pretending and wanting to fit in and please others. Years of psychotherapy training and my own therapy work escaped me. Years of coaching others to honor and respect their boundaries escaped me.

The ground rule of saying "yes" only when you mean "yes" and "no" when you need to say "no" escaped me. I faked it.

It was a very long and painful hour that quite quickly and efficiently brought to the surface my lifelong confusion about being able to advocate for myself in sexual situations. I did not want to be high maintenance. I wanted to fit in. I wanted to please others. I wanted to be liked. But really, what did I want? Could I be authentic about my needs and get what I wanted? The larger question was, "Can I be authentic in the world and have it turn out well?" Because I hadn't been authentic (beginning with the attempted manipulation of the group and ending with pretending with these men who deserved more from me) I really could not answer these questions.

I left the exercise feeling shaken and fragile, and when I was alone, I broke down in tears—lots of tears.

I found Ken and told him how miserable the experience had been.

"Why didn't you just say 'No thank you' to erotic play with those men?"

I exploded. "Oh, come on! No one is saying 'no' at this workshop! The whole culture of Tantra this weekend has been to say 'yes!'" I felt right and pleased with myself for finally standing up for myself.

He challenged me a bit sternly. "You don't know what would have happened if you said 'No.' You could have changed the culture of the workshop. You chose not to, experimented with not saying 'No.' You also experimented with 'pretending' in an erotic situation. Now that you have the data from these experiments, you can make different decisions next time."

*Right.* Everything *is an experiment.*

He was right, but I didn't feel any better.

Clearly, I had some desire to pretend, or I would not have done it. The point of the workshop was to be conscious about both our desires and pursuit of said desires. I quickly realized that pretending did not feel good. It felt downright ugly and sickening.

Later, when I was feeling a little less sorry for myself, I complained to Ken, "Why can't I learn these lessons through having hot sex?"

He laughed. "You already know how to have hot sex. Now you need to learn how to access your erotic energy outside the context of hot sex. Remember: everything, *everything* is an experiment. Tantra isn't about faith—I don't need you to believe anything. The point is to experience, evaluate, under-

stand, and learn. Good job gathering the data for this experiment."

I wanted to say, "Fuck you," but chuckled. He knew what
I wanted to say.

We'd made an agreement as a group at the start of the
workshop to refrain from drinking alcohol and using drugs
over the weekend. Even though I'm not a big drinker, that
evening I really craved a drink. I was really shaken. I sheepishly admitted my desire to Ken.

"Have one. Have a strong one. Enjoy it, and gather the
data!"

There really is no concept of right and wrong in this tradition.

Zachary and I went out to dinner and ordered a couple of
martinis. Zachary was always ready to break a rule. We shared
more about our days with each other, and I started to feel
better. I wasn't a blubbering idiot that often. He appreciated
the opportunity to take care of me, and I loved letting him.

And the martini, with a splash of St. Germain, was delicious.

# CHAPTER 4

*Not only did my husband die, but he remained dead.*

— *Anonymous blog post*

*Every desire of your body is holy; Every desire of your body is Holy*

— *Hafiz*

I WAS STUNNED when I stumbled upon this blog post shortly after Zachary's death. Those words are so real. His death was a devastating trauma to my system and our community of family and friends—but over the days and weeks that followed a whole new trauma emerged for me: he remained dead. Living my life as the calendar pages continued turning was incredibly challenging.

Others around us slowly (and not so slowly) returned to their normal, unchanged lives. But for Zoe and me, the painful truth was that he remained dead. This realization emerged and reemerged in a myriad of ways, times, and places.

The night Zachary died, I had been in shock. I was barely functioning, but immediately below the surface, I was breaking apart. After Ken brought me home from the hospital and was in and out of my house that first full day, he offered to come back early the following morning. Because I knew I needed something but had no idea what it might be, I agreed.

Over the previous year, as Ken's student in Tantra, he'd helped me process a lot of vulnerable emotions and psychological debris. I'd dealt with fears of dying, of parenting, of living large, of getting what I wanted, of not getting what I wanted. I'd worked on my body shame and insecurities. At the time of Zachary's death, I trusted Ken to be with my emotional self. That foundation of trust made it possible for me to lean on him in the hours, days, and weeks after the trauma.

Ken arrived at my house at 6:00 the next morning with an open heart and a lot of courage. Many of my loved ones were afraid of my intense grief, but Ken was not—he was not tentative with me. Other close loved ones were too mired in their own grief over their loss of Zachary and in their own feelings of powerlessness to help Zoe or me with our grief.

A friend was asleep on the living room couch, and Zoe was asleep in my bed when I tiptoed through the living room to let Ken in. We quietly made cups of steaming chai tea and retreated to the unfinished basement for privacy. There was a ratty red couch, decades-old wall-to-wall carpet, and a huge hand-me-down TV. There was no mistaking this room for anything but a basement in a home built almost one hundred years earlier. I sat on the cold floor and cried while Ken held me.

I wasn't just crying or even sobbing; I was wracked with physical pain. I felt like my stomach had been kicked hard and I was on the verge of vomiting. My chest hurt as if my lungs were being squeezed from the inside. I was short of breath. Snot was flowing. This outpouring of grief went on for two to three hours. My body felt rigid like I was fighting death.

Nothing about the experience felt pleasurable to me—not that morning, and not the many mornings later when Ken and I repeated this ritual.

After several hours of tears and pain, I realized that Zoe would wake up soon. I knew that I both wanted to, and had to be at least somewhat available to her as she woke up on this first day without her other dad. I had heard too many stories from clients who had lost a parent during childhood. Their surviving parent had been lost to them as well, too lost in their own grief to help their frightened child(ren). I did not want to be that parent for my tender, broken-hearted girl.

I drew on all of my strength and reserves and forced myself to stop crying. To my surprise, I discovered that I felt just a little more open and clearer than I had a couple of hours earlier. I had some confidence that I could welcome Zoe to the day and be just stable enough to parent her.

*Why do I feel more open? Are we doing Tantra? What the fuck is Tantra in the face of raw grief and death?*

I had learned a lot from Ken before we arrived at that moment. I had discovered that in the process of practicing Tantra a lot of intense energy is generated. These energies, generated at each of the body's energy centers, called "chakras," are palpable. Each center is associated with various and specific psychological, spiritual, physical, and emotional issues. I knew enough at that point to know that I was experiencing and somehow engaging with pain in my belly and heart chakras. The rest of my subtle energetic body was not all that accessible to me. But my heart (fourth chakra) and my belly (third chakra) were definitely engaged and felt broken, radiating pain.

Somehow, my crying and writhing had released energy, allowing it to flow up and down my chakra/energetic system. This movement is why I felt more open after hours of crying. The pain in my body, which had felt entirely static, permanent, and relentless, was moving. Energy can hurt like hell as it moves; an endless supply of pain seemed to be filling my belly and my heart, yet the energy was somehow no longer stuck. I knew from studying psychology that stuck grief wreaks havoc on one's life. This first morning I had my first glimpse how dynamic and alive grief was in my body.

Zachary had been dead for thirty hours, and I was in my unfinished basement practicing Tantra because it was the only thing I could think of that might help. Of course, at the time I did not know I was practicing Tantra; that only became clear in hindsight. I was just trusting my body and allowing it do do what it needed: to cry. I was practicing Tantra, with no sex and no orgasm, intensely crying, which was moving energy throughout my body. Counterintuitively, I began to experience a feeling of increased freedom. Feeling energy move, I viscerally understood that the agony I was experiencing didn't have to stay stuck. It could move. I trusted that it would move.

This understanding didn't lessen my pain; I felt no relief. But I felt reassured that the pain was not permanent and could change. Ken created a container for my pain with his kindness and steady presence. I was able to unleash the profoundly awful energy of grief because I trusted his ability to contain and hold it well.

I was not pretty. Even though I showered and brushed my teeth, I smelled like death and could barely eat. I was sweating, crying, and full of snot. While I am guessing he felt some fear at having me collapse in his arms, Ken did not let his fear get in the way of his ability to maintain a physical container for me. The container we created was solid then because we had luckily been creating it during the year before Zachary's death.

After that first Tantra workshop, I had decided that I wanted to work individually with Ken. Zachary had already had several one-on-one sessions with Ken, which complicated our monogamy agreement. We'd had lengthy discussions about what being in erotic space with someone else (Ken) without the other present would mean to our relationship. It was not something we had done before, and at first, I was uncomfortable making another change in the container that worked for us so well.

I wanted us both to be present for the other's work with Ken to keep our container more or less intact. But Zachary preferred to do his personal work separately. I had to sit with my uncomfortable feelings.

As I did, I realized that while erotic, these sacred erotic sessions with Ken were not about having sex with him but about accessing our own erotic energy and experimenting with how to use that energy to heal emotionally and psychologically. The goal of the sessions was to develop our relationship with the sacred, with God. Ken wasn't going to be Zachary's (or my) fuck buddy. Rather, he was what I would call an erotic therapist—a sacred intimate. I trusted the three of us to engage with one another openly and intimately without creating the drama of a triangle.

Ken was not looking to leave his marriage, and neither Zachary nor I was looking for a boyfriend on the side. We were all aware that we were playing with intense eroticism coupled with emotional vulnerability, which required us all to have solid boundaries and impeccable integrity.

Ken had reminded me that a session without Zachary present would be an experiment. We all acknowledged that it would be different for each of us and that we would try to stay aware and conscious of whatever emerged—in Ken's words, "We would gather the data from the experiment."

Ken and I began to meet a few times a month, and I started engaging with the principles of Tantra as Ken explained them to me. During my first session with Ken, he brought up his fee. Talking about my paying him led me to share my relationship with money and how financially overextended I was at that time. I started to feel sad and scared.

Ken listened thoughtfully and explained, "Money issues are often related to the first and third chakras. These chakras are connected with survival and our ability to be authentic in our every day lives. Erotic play can help create a bridge between these two chakras—through the second chakra." As I was trying to understand this new and seemingly bizarre concept intellectually, he knew I was trying to formulate a question that would help me master this in my brain. Instead of waiting for my question he offered to suck my dick. He instructed me to try to simultaneously feel the pleasure of his sucking with the sadness and fear of all things money that was buried in me.

"Feel the pleasure and the fear together," he suggested. "They are not mutually exclusive."

This time was the first I had considered that we can feel emotional pain and physical pleasure concurrently, rather than seeking or using pleasure to mask, avoid, or take a break from emotional pain.

This concept of the mutual experience of pleasure and pain would become a foundation of our work together for the next several years.

During that first experiment with emotional pain and physical pleasure, I was simultaneously aware of both the pleasure of my cock in his mouth and my anxiety surrounding money. An unexpected sadness gurgled inside. I'm not sure where this fascinating exercise would have taken me because a minute later, we both smelled smoke. When Ken had taken off his shirt, he'd carelessly tossed it behind him, and it had landed on a candle and caught fire! Ken put out the fire and told me that on the night of his first session with his teacher, he and his teacher had started a fire in their hotel room in just the same way—clothes thrown onto a lit candle.

Ken opened the window and the air in the room cleared and cooled. I watched him vacuuming the room, I felt like I was in a trance. I still felt the sadness that had started to gurgle up during the blow job. After the vacuum was put away, Ken noticed that I was distressed and came over to hold me. At first, I was shaking from the cold, but then the shaking came from deep inside. I was scared and sad.

Ken took off his clothes to meet me in my state of undress and held me in his arms, skin to skin, as we talked. He asked me to stay aware of what I was feeling and where the energy was in my body. Ken was incredibly loving and healing and reassuring. I felt held in a profoundly deep way. I realized that my desire to be authentic, to feel like it was perfectly okay to be me, meant that I had to be as accepting and loving and healing and reassuring with myself as Ken was with me.

During the first year of my Tantric study with Ken, my body behaved in a way that was unfamiliar; most often I was not able to get or maintain an erection. I had been frustrated. When Zachary and I had engaged erotically together, my erections had been as I had expected: easily accessible and not an issue. When we engaged in a Tantra setting, I was not hard—really ever.

So by this time, I no longer trusted my body-specifically my cock. I thought I needed and knew I wanted a hard cock to engage erotically. I felt betrayed by my body, believing that my brain knew more.

Being sexual without an erection for the better part of a year opened a new window to engage erotically. During erotic play with Ken (even when Zachary was present) I was quite turned on but often did not have an erection. *How can I completely enjoy this sexual play and not be hard?* I regarded this new bodily quirk as a handicap in my Tantric study. I felt inadequate—as though I were trying to swim with my hands tied together.

"Trust your body and trust your cock." Ken reminded me when I was feeling pouty or sullen about my soft cock. "There is information in your soft cock."

*Easy for you to say.*

# CHAPTER 5

*People do not die for us immediately, but remain bathed
in a sort of aura of life which bears no relation to true
immortality but through which they continue to occupy
our thoughts in the same way as when they were alive.
It is as though they were traveling abroad.*

—Marcel Proust

IN THE DAYS and weeks after Zachary's death, I tried to
think of ways that I could help Zoe engage with her grief.
Kids, I observed, do not immediately get hit with grief the
way adults do.

Even though our community of grieving adults did our best
to make room for our children's feelings, the kids who loved
Zachary were not crying like the adults. Their experience with
grief seemed to me more like a tsunami that began with just a
bit of water creeping in under the door. Over time their collective grief gained speed and eventually crashed down the door.

Zoe's grief was different—more like a nagging trickle. At
times she was just a bit off center—and at other times she was
entirely overwhelmed.

Even years later, when going to sleep, starting a new activity, new school, or other unpredictable times, her grief would

hit in a massive wave, and she would cry uncontrollably about something small, and then say, "I miss Daddy."

The morning after the accident, the trauma raw for everyone, Zoe seemed disoriented and tentative. Thinking I needed to do something to be helpful, I suggested she and I smudge the house. We burned sage and myrrh around all of the doors, windows, as well as the perimeter of the house. While we burned the herbs, we talked about letting Daddy's energy go to where it and he needed to go. I had no idea what to say during this ritual, but she and I used the smoke and our house tour to begin to figure out a language to talk about death, and loss, and missing someone we loved.

As a family, we didn't tend to display photos around the house. Recently, though, we had placed a framed 8"x12" photograph of Zoe and Zachary on the fireplace mantle; they were in the school parking lot, wearing their matching (red) school T-shirts. During our house tour, and seemingly out of nowhere, Zoe found one of Zachary's muddy work boots and placed it on the mantle, next to their photograph. We had created an altar; I added his keys, his phone, and his wedding band, which were still in the ziplock bag given to me at the hospital. We gathered some photographs, his passport, wallet, day minder, eyeglasses, and neatly arranged them on our mantle. Zoe asked if she could have his phone. I said she could.

Over the coming weeks, we each added items to the altar. More pictures appeared, as did small stuffed animals, little toys, and some sea glass from our collection. Zoe often arranged and re-arranged items calmly and easily. She was interacting with her loss in ways that made sense to her.

The therapist in me was relieved to see her physically working with Daddy's things as a way of unpacking what this loss meant to her. I knew that I wanted her to be pro-foundly affected by this loss because I knew all too well that if she were not, her grief would show up later in life and wreak havoc in subtle and not subtle ways.

There is no escaping the magnitude of the death of a parent on a six-year-old. As a grieving spouse and parent to a dev-astated child, I was heartbroken to see her "working" with her grief. Before this moment, I had struggled with my feel-ings of powerlessness when my tiny daughter had a gas pain, and I could do nothing to comfort her. Now, watching her try to digest something as life-altering as the death of her parent was unbearable.

At times, friends or family members contributed small items to our altar. Whenever one of those arrived, Zoe would notice and make sure I noticed. We used these items to begin telling stories about Daddy. To this day, whenever we are with his family and friends who knew us as a family of three, the Zachary stories flow.

The altar stayed up for a month or so. One day I was talking with a mom who had adopted a kid from China. She told me that her Chinese daughter kept a "China Box" under her bed with all of the memorabilia from her orphan-age, China, her parents' trip to get her, and pictures of her early caregivers. I liked that idea so, when we dismantled the altar, Zoe and I created a "Daddy Box."

Today these things still reside in her Daddy Box, which she stores under her bed. From time to time, I notice that the box has been opened and things have been touched.

*He remains dead.*

Somehow, these rituals helped Zoe be more present and engaged in what we were all experiencing. We often repeated our smudging ritual alone and with friends those first weeks and months. Zoe seemed more at ease when we invited our friends to participate. Having our pain witnessed was somehow comforting to her.

In the song "Sometime Around Midnight," by *Airborne Toxic Event*, the lyrics describe a change of emotion when memories return like "feral waves" and "being lost in a haze of wine." This was my experience. In my case, the haze was brutal, raw, relentless grief. I wished it were the wine.

Smudging helped me bridge the gap between being lost and homeless and providing home and hope for my frightened six-year-old daughter. At the same time, I was fighting, welcoming, engaging with, submitting to, and being fucked by waves of memories. I was most certainly lost in the haze. We were, at times, both lost in the haze.

On Tuesday of the first full day after Zachary's death, Zoe requested that we move her bed into my room. No, she did not want to sleep in my bed; she wanted her bed in my room.

How could I say no? For years we'd trusted her to tell us what she needed. We'd trusted her about when to stop wearing diapers, what foods she wanted to eat, and where she wanted to sleep. Of course I trusted her desire to have her bed in my room. A group of us, led by Zoe, moved her bed into my tiny bedroom. With about fourteen inches between our two beds, she ultimately moved into my bed altogether.

At night, she needed me to lie down with her for her to fall asleep. She needed songs, stories, cuddling, and ritual to relax enough to nod off. Her grief broke my heart. She'd always been relaxed at bedtime and quick to fall asleep. It was not lost on me that just a few nights before, she'd gone to sleep and woken up with her daddy dead, her papa a wreck, and her world stunned and saddened.

These were my days: a haze of people, food, tears, details, calls. And each day, Ken showed up at 6:00 in the morning. We drank our tea, went down to the basement and sat on the red couch, where he held me, and I cried—for hours. After I cried, I felt some sense of relief—enough to attend to my day as a grieving single parent of a grieving child. Repeat daily. Repeat daily. Repeat daily.

I was just barely functioning, and had to make big decisions. How long could I stay out of work? School was starting in three weeks, and I had no idea how I was going to get Zoe to school. This question seemed urgent. Did I need a nanny? What was my life going to look like? What school should Zoe attend? *Can I do it? Can I really do this?* I had never been this frightened.

Ken coached me to trust what I wanted, regardless of how crazy or impractical or complex. Trust my desire—trust that the thoughts, ideas, and desires that emerged from my body are what is best for me. This trust of one's body is the essence of Tantra. I just didn't know that then.

At first, I thought I wanted and needed a nanny to drive Zoe to and from school so I could continue my role in the family as the guy who brought in the money. Zachary had died, yes, but we still had multiple mortgages and other bills that required my attention and, more to the point, money.

Hiring a nanny seemed like a plan, and I felt some relief that I had one. A friend took on the task of writing the ad for a nanny. A tiny glimpse into my new life was emerging.

But through my mindful crying jags, as energy moved in my body and allowed some of the pain to move, I realized my desires were changing. My thinking was changing. The plan I had thought was right no longer was. I noticed a different desire beginning to emerge. Moving energy in my body via my rather unsexy crying allowed me to know what I wanted. Moving my pain allowed me to experience more freedom in my thinking.

I was surprised to discover that I wanted to be the person who drove Zoe to school, and I wanted to be the person who picked her up. I wanted to be a stay-at-home dad. It took a couple of weeks (which felt like months) of crying and experiencing myself in my body to find that clarity and know that was what I really wanted.

*Really, I just want him not to be dead.*

Not hiring a nanny turned out to be best for Zoe. I soon realized that taking her to school and picking her up also helped to move me out of my haze of grief. We had to be in the car by 7:10 AM and I needed to be back at school at 3:00 PM. It was a basic routine that I could build my life around. My new life was beginning to emerge.

I trusted my desire to be with Zoe. I reached back to my early understanding of Tantra and the pleasure principle— trust desire. Deep pleasures lead to deep healing. I wanted to be at home and to be a full-time Papa. I sensed, given our givens, that although a wreck, I could find deep pleasure in being Zoe's full-time Papa, shepherding her into her new life.

There was one small problem with my desire: I couldn't afford it. While Zachary and I planned carefully for what would happen in the event of our deaths, we'd made the conscious decision not to insure his life. Zachary was younger, stronger, and more fit than I, so it seemed unlikely that he would die first. And besides, I was the primary breadwinner, and we both trusted my ability to make money. This plan neglected one small but crucial point: I would be a complete mess and unable to work if my husband died. Even though

I am a therapist (with a Master's degree in grief and loss), somehow, my probable inability to function should he predecease me never occurred to me.

Everyone kept asking what they could do to help. Many people showed up with food, but grief drove away my appetite, and I was physically unable to eat much.

"If you need anything... just ask."

*How many times had I heard this?*

I was frustrated. Just as I became clear on my desire to be with Zoe these next months, the financial reality seemingly derailed executing this plan. I reverted back to my well-worn narrative: "I cannot get what I want." While sharing this frustration with Ken, he recalled that whenever he was stuck, he went back to the Tantric principles. Trusting my desire didn't seem to be panning out for me. He gently reminded me to trust my desire.

*Does he actually believe this?*

My desire to take some time to be with Zoe stayed steady. I trusted that this desire was real and right. Then, seemingly out of nowhere—after a particularly wretched crying jag—came an idea.

*If you need anything... anything... just ask.*

With much humility, I asked for money. I explained that I wanted to have the time to learn how to be Zoe's full-time Papa while we were both intensely grieving. I wanted to have time with her to shepherd her through this huge transition. I wanted to help her grieve knowing that her process might parallel my process yet would be distinctly different. I wanted to learn how to make her lunch. I wanted to find some ease with her. I wanted some time for myself to navigate this morass of pain, hurt, confusion, fear, and deep longing.

Time was my greatest need and desire.

With help and encouragement from friends, I wrote a note that explained what I wanted and needed. When people asked what I needed, friends and family made sure they got a copy of the letter.

I am embarrassed to admit that I was not yet aware of the fact that I couldn't have gone back to work even if I had wanted to. There was simply no way I could have attended to anyone else's story, pain, or needs besides my own and Zoe's. In the wake of Zachary's death, I had lost my ability to be anyone's therapist. Nanny or no nanny, money or no money, I had to stay at home (my career was now another powerful thread of loss).

Family, friends, and, most surprisingly, acquaintances and strangers gave me money.

Some people gave me a surprising amount of money and others gave less. Over a hundred people gave me money. Those who could not give money took care of my garden, cleaned my house, washed my car, or just sat with me when I needed company. My counselor did not charge me for six months of sessions. I was shocked and grateful. I was loved and felt loved.

My plan worked! I was able to keep Zoe and myself comfortably afloat for those first six months until I was able to creep back into my therapist chair.

While it was the most painful time in my life, having the time to feel and process this trauma was the most significant gift I could have received. It was also deeply pleasurable to have time to feel, breathe deeply, walk, visit loved ones, and process what had happened to Zachary and us. Without that time, I would have gotten stuck in the pain, lost in the haze. Allowing myself the time to feel my pain, and feel it intensely, was oddly pleasurable—I was awake and alive. It wasn't fun pleasure, rather the pleasure of feeling alive (no small feat given the state I was in). Feeling awake and alive in the wake of traumatic and sudden death and loss was the most overwhelming and profound paradox I had ever experienced. It was also how I learned, really learned, the principles and practices of Tantra.

The time I had with Zoe was deeply healing. She and I navigated the ups and downs creating a wholly different life than we had had just a short time before. We were father and daughter. We were a single-parent family who was missing Zachary.

I trusted my desire. I asked for what I wanted—and to my astonishment, trusting my desire and asking for what I wanted worked.

# CHAPTER 6

*Here is the world. Beautiful and terrible things will
happen. Don't be afraid.*

—*Frederick Buechner*

BEFORE ZACHARY DIED, we were one of those lucky
families who did not struggle with the details of our day-to-
day lives. Our division of labor and tasks felt good to each
of us. Much of the ease stemmed from the fact that Zachary
was a teacher at Zoe's school, so they commuted together
and had the same schedule. We rarely had the usual kid-care
scramble other families regularly experience. We so appreciated and rarely took for granted the ease we had created.

But the details of what was our simple life became daunting
once they were all placed in my lap—overwhelming, in fact.

For Zoe and me, the change in our relationship went
beyond our mutual grief over Zachary's death. While I was
an engaged, connected parent, I had never been the one to get
her ready for school. I did not get breakfast ready for her car
ride. I did not make her lunch or pack her bag. I did not get
her dressed. I did not sign enrollment forms. I did not track
immunization forms. I did not gather the stuff for emergency
kits for school. I did not do back-to-school shopping. I did
not carry her asleep from her bed to the car.

I hugged her, took her to the park, read to her, bathed her, fed her, laughed with her, talked with her, held her, and loved her. I have no doubt she felt loved and deeply connected with me. But I'd had Zachary to co-parent with me. She had two dads. Now on my own, I was overwhelmed and terrified in a way that I had never experienced.

Friends kept reassuring me that I was not alone, lots of people would help. While all of that was kind and true to an extent, a part of me knew that mine was a solo journey. I had to delve into the depths of my pain, insecurity, and fear to find the strength, creativity, and life force to heal myself and shepherd Zoe into her new life.

Sadly, I was right. I was on a solo journey. Zachary was gone, and the details of our lives were left for me to handle. Somehow, over those first few weeks, I made decisions and kept going, but I was only making decisions when they needed to be made. I had no awareness of the future beyond any particular decision. I only could focus on what was before me; everything else was a blur.

At first, friends and family slept at the house with us because I had no idea what I needed or what might crop up in the middle of some night. I was clearly not ready to be the only adult in the house. While having friends around was comforting, it was also disorienting. Everything was disorienting.

After those first weeks, I decided to stop having people stay over, and asked that people stop bringing over pans of casseroles and dishes of baked goods. The time had arrived for Zoe and me to begin the next step in our journey. For those outside of my inner circle, our inner circle, life returned to normal. And the house became quiet—very quiet.

Not only would Zoe begin first grade three weeks after Zachary's death, but he was also supposed to be her first-grade teacher that year. They had both been excited. In fact, they had each been looking forward to this year for the previous four years. *How do I manage this?*

Their school was in a smaller city that was a forty-five—minute drive from home. They'd commuted together for the last four years. During the ride they listened to audio books (*Harry Potter* and *The Chronicles of Narnia* were their favorites); Zoe ate breakfast and napped. At their school, I was known as the husband of the hippest, funniest, and all-around favorite teacher. While I was liked by all and loved by many, these were not my people. They were Zachary's people.

With Zachary gone, it was completely impractical for Zoe to attend school so far from home. As the beginning of school approached, I mulled over the dilemma trying to create sensible options. There appeared to be none.

Then it hit me: the staff and kids at her school were not only Zachary's people, but they were also Zoe's people. She had been part of that school's community for the previous four years. Zoe needed to be there while she grieved. The staff knew and loved her, the kids all knew and loved her, and my gut feeling was that it would be a good place for her to grieve and heal, or at least to begin her life-long journey of grief and healing.

I had no idea how this would all work. The forty-five-to fifty-five-minute drive to, and from, school overwhelmed me. The prospect of that same commute in the morning and afternoon made my brain hurt. But I was certain that she needed to be there, and I trusted myself to figure it all out in the coming weeks.

My gut sense about what was best for her was spot on. She needed to be there. Her grief was welcome at her school. In fact, her grief was a part of a whole community that was shocked, saddened, and shaken by Zachary's sudden death. Her school community grieved with her. The first week of school the kids in all grades participated (according to his or her connection with Zachary and desire to join) in an activity contemplating Zachary and death. Each child drew, wrote, talked, or created something while figuring out a way to say goodbye. For many of the children, losing this favorite teacher was their first experience with death.

The staff, as individuals and collectively, made room for Zoe—her strength, her struggles, her history, and her grief, as well as for other kids' reactions and feelings. The staff was wise enough to also make room for their own profound shock and sadness, as well as for mine and other adults touched by Zachary's passing.

They were kind and gracious when, at drop-off or pick-up, I burst into tears. I received hugs. I got food. I shared tears with other parents and staff. They allowed and encouraged Zoe to take walks with the gym teacher and her big black lab to just talk. The Head of School encouraged Zoe to use her office as a place of refuge when she was overwhelmed, wanted to talk, or just needed quiet.

At the end of the first week, the school held a memorial service honoring Zachary. Families, friends, and others in the school community gathered in the schoolyard to remember Zachary as a friend, teacher, father, and family member. When they released a single helium balloon with all the students' names painstakingly written on its tail, I was simultaneously touched and crushed. For them, school would return to a new normal next week. But I had no idea what or where Zoe's new normal would be or when it might arrive.

# CHAPTER 7

*It kills me sometimes, how people die.*
*—Markus Zusak, The Book Thief*

DEATH MADE MY world small. I was very aware that there was a world around me, but I had little interest or motivation to participate in it. I only had energy for engaging with my inner world and with Zoe and her world.

*He remains dead.*

My husband remained dead. Each day, I came face to face with this reality. I knew in my head that Zachary was no longer alive, but I still felt energetically tied to him. I felt he should be right next to me. My hand kept reaching out to touch him; my eyes searched for him, my ears listened for his footsteps. I could hear him laugh. I could hear him call me. I could feel him in bed next to me. I heard his car pulling into the driveway. I touched my wedding ring with my thumb as I had done for the last nine years. My mind remembered that he was gone, but my body still hadn't caught up to this new reality.

Spiritual and religious traditions try to make sense of the mystery of death. Who dies when, and how, and why?

Nothing I had heard before Zachary's death really made sense. The best sense I could make of it was to accept that I couldn't question 'God's will,' but I was responsible for showing up when life became challenging. I don't believe we are responsible for creating our illnesses or our deaths or other things that happen to us, but we are responsible to them. We are called to show up for whatever happens and attend to the hardships, including deaths.

*Simple, right?*

I was responsible for showing up to the reality that my beloved was dead. *Gone. Forever.*

That night in the hospital, I committed to 'just' show up and be as present as I knew how to be. Showing up to my grief and pain was not an easy task; it meant hurting most of the day, every day. But that is what I did. It was all I knew to do.

In hindsight, it seems clear, even to my incredibly logical and concrete-thinking mind, that Zachary and I knew on some level that he was going to die soon. There are many things about the months (and even years) before his death that convince me that this was so.

Zachary never made physical mistakes. He could climb, use a chainsaw on one foot, lift, walk across rooftops, balance and work on ladders, and he never got hurt. He could go from a season of couch potato to running ten miles in a day and not be sore. He was in his body in such a way that he kept himself well and safe. He was strong and coordinated. Might running into the road, into oncoming traffic, have been his first physical mistake? I am suspicious that it was not a mistake but part of some fucked-up plan.

On the morning of his death, we were sitting on the dock at our friend's lake cabin having a lovely, easy morning. Seemingly out of nowhere, over a cup of coffee, Zachary hopped up and said, "I'm 39 and I'm afraid I'm going to die soon. I'm going to join a gym."

I chuckled as I noticed the beautiful dance his shirtless muscular torso did as he moved toward the phone. He called a gym and joined right then and there—because he was afraid he was going to die. *Soon.*

Zachary was fit, lean, strong, and muscular (and he never worked out, which was more than annoying). He had perfect blood pressure and no health risk factors. That he was "afraid to die" on that particular morning was odd at best. Odd, but it was also very Zachary. He did have a flair for the dramatic.

Later that day, again seemingly out of nowhere, our friend Nancy said the word "widow" while relating a family story. I hadn't heard that word in years.

Six-year-old Zoe asked me, "Papa, what is a widow?"

I explained that if one's spouse dies, one becomes a widow. Then I added, "If Daddy died, I would become a widow." It felt funny at that moment to use such a close-to-home example to define that word for my daughter, but it also seemed like the best way to describe that particular word to Zoe.

Zachary looked at me sharply (with a hint of his wry smile—we were kind of word snobs together) and corrected me. "Widower."

He had corrected me about seven hours before I became one.

When we had met nearly fifteen years earlier, we'd spent the first five months of our relationship as more-or-less fuck buddies. We had a twenty-four-hour date once a week and a quick phone-chat midweek.

It was sexy and fun. On one of these dates, we'd had a bit too much to drink and got to talking. We agreed that our dates were becoming more like boyfriend dates as opposed to fuck buddy dates. Zachary said that he was afraid to get closer to me because he was afraid that I was going to die. He was twenty-five when he said this and I was thirty-three.

The next day, I was in an accident where I did almost die.

To access my home from the garage I had to take a tram (a funicular of sorts) up and down the hill. It rode on railroad tracks. Because it was mildly scary for me, and terrifying for first timers, I often rode with them up and down the hill.

Zachary had just left my home after one of our twenty-four-hour dates. Jesse was the new dog in my life, and a friend came over to meet her. As I was taking my friend up the hill, Jesse escaped the house (through the cat door!) and started to run up the tracks after us. She had her leash on and it got caught and I saw her neck was being pulled under the front wheel. Frantic, I lunged for her and managed to unclip her leash before she got hurt—but in the process, I tumbled onto the tracks and the tram ran over me.

I only vaguely remember being airlifted to the trauma center in Seattle. I spent nineteen days in the hospital with a broken pelvis and other injuries. It was not clear I would survive the night and for the first few days of that hospitalization, I didn't know if I would walk again. Zachary spent every one of those days with me. That is where we started to fall in love.

About 10 days after my injury, as I was stabilizing, his therapist asked Zachary if I was able to have erections. Zachary came to the hospital to find out.

He asked me if I'd had an erection since the injury and I sheepishly said "no." Given how I felt, the eggplant-purple color of my bruised and swollen cock and balls, lack of access to showers and toilets, and being confined to a hospital bed, erections were not really on my mind.

Today, they were on his mind. He closed the curtains around my bed, dropped his pants, and revealed his brand new foreskin piercing (which was quite a handsome addition to an already pretty and perfect penis) and got to touching my black-and-blue cock and balls. Although painful, I was able to get and maintain an erection, for which both of us were grateful.

Once I was discharged from the hospital, I needed around-the-clock care, and Zachary spent his non-working time doing just that. He even took time away from work to be the lynchpin of my home care. In effect, he moved in with me.

He moved into what became our home because I had saved a dog. We often wondered if we would still be together had I not saved our dog from an almost certain and ugly death.

Zachary was killed attempting to save our dog from an almost certain and ugly death in four lanes of traffic. Coincidental? I don't think so, although I have no idea about what the deeper meaning is.

Almost five years to the day before he was killed, we were sitting on the porch at home surrounded by tiny Zoe, three old dogs, and three old cats. Zachary looked at me in a way I can remember so clearly as though it were yesterday and said, "I wonder who will be here five years from now?"

We both knew he was referring to our aging animals, but now I wonder. The vividness with which I remember the question makes me wonder if he, or we, knew something at a subconscious level.

About a year into my study of Tantra with Ken (before Zachary's death) I became ill. It was nothing serious, but I let myself worry that I might be seroconverting. Even though I hadn't been engaging in high-risk sexual behaviors, and even though I know that seroconversion does not mean death, I was convinced I was dying.

I decided to look at my fear of dying in the context of Tantra. Ken and I dove into my fear and explored it in my body. I looked deeply into my faith that if I were to die, it would all be okay—for me, for Zoe, and for Zachary. This exploration began two months before Zachary died. Although I didn't explore the possibility of Zachary dying, every day during those months preceding his death, I was working with my fear of my death and dying.

Zachary's father died when Zachary was seven; his mom died when he was fifteen. When Zoe turned six, Zachary began remembering how sick his father had been when he was six. He began to talk seriously about his fear of dying in therapy and at home with me. He talked at an intense and deep level about what it was like for him to lose his dad that young. His family did not talk much about his dad's sickness, impending death, or even his death after the fact.

Zachary recounted the story of going to school the day after his dad died and how utterly disorienting that was. He wanted to resolve his unexamined feelings about his dad's death so that when Zoe was seven (the age he was when his dad died), he could be free of these lingering issues.

About a week before Zachary's death, he was in his counselor's office talking about his fears around his death; I was working with Ken on my own fears around my death, and Zoe was asking about the details of the deaths of our three dogs that had passed in the last year. Leo (our pug) had died just four days before this conversation. So there we were, all of us processing fears, thoughts, and reactions to death a week before Zachary died.

NOT TOO LONG before moving into our new house in the city, I began to experience what I assumed to be irrational fear when Zachary went out for an evening walk: I was afraid for his life. I feared he was going to die each time he left the house in the evening. He knew I had this fear, my therapist knew I had this fear, and our close friends knew about this fear. This fear was stark, recurrent, and was specific: Zachary would die when it was dark, and he was alone and when he was out walking. And it was death I predicted: not injury, not violence, but death. I felt no anxiety when he was with a friend, in a car, or out in the day.

I no longer feel this fear about anyone else. That fear has completely vanished.

I also had long-running panic when Zachary did not answer his phone at times when I thought he should be available (like when he was driving home from work). When he did not answer his phone at those times, I immediately assumed he was dead. *Dead.* Not injured, not on the other line, and not otherwise engaged. *Dead.* We both thought this fear was based on my anxiety and need for control. I no longer think that it was.

The day he was killed, he'd wanted to stay another night at Nancy's cabin, but I wanted to leave, and it took some negotiation before he agreed. The odd thing was that from the moment we decided to leave, he took over. He decided when we were leaving the cabin so we could avoid the traffic of weekend vacationers heading back to the city—and was quite smug about his ability to choose the fastest routes with the fewest traffic delays. During the car ride, Zachary, Nancy, and I talked about how we were in the middle of doing all of this psychological/spiritual work with our respective mentors about death and our fears of death. It was a very intense and moving conversation, and we all felt close. We talked about trusting life and having faith that we are not in charge of life. We even discussed that if one of us were to die or face some misfortune, we would all know how to show up and regroup and have a good life.

We also discussed dinner plans. I wanted to stop on the way to have dinner, but Zachary vetoed that; he wanted to head back to our neighborhood. I acquiesced and named a restaurant I wanted to go to near home, but he wanted to go to another. Usually, he was easygoing about restaurants, schedules, and driving decisions. He was quite different that afternoon; I cannot remember another time when he said 'no' to a restaurant suggestion. Nancy, Zachary, and I all noted this difference. We even laughed about it.

After dinner, he dropped off Nancy, drove us home, set Zoe up with her movie, and left for his ill-fated walk with the dog. Once he announced his evening stroll, I felt my all-too-familiar fear.

It almost seemed like he was driven to get himself to the place where he would be struck by the car. Uncharacteristically, he'd taken charge of our journey. During the the last six hours of his life, he had somehow delivered himself to the street where not one, but two, street lights were out, and where three of four lanes of traffic stopped when a small dog got out of his control at the very moment an unsuspecting driver of a Honda CR-V came barreling down the fourth lane at forty-three miles-an-hour.

There were other strange occurrences. The week before he died, Zachary was at school getting ready for the start of the school year. His best friend at school, Vic, told me that Zachary was uncharacteristically disengaged and disconnected during their conversation. Normally Zachary made you feel like you were the most important person in the world to him. Vic did not feel his familiar vibe on that particular day.

On his way out of school, a different teacher asked him if he would be in on Tuesday. Zachary replied, "Yeah, I'll see you Tuesday... or not." His answer struck her as odd and uncharacteristic. He had every conscious intention of being at school Tuesday—of that I am certain. And yet he said, "... or not."

We had attended a Tantra workshop a few months before he died where our group assignment was to define a personal issue that got in the way of us living the lives we wanted. We then created erotic experiments to see if we could learn something about ourselves, our habits, and the issue itself. I decided to work on my distorted body image. I felt fat.

My experiment was to stand naked in front of my fellow Tantric explorers and somehow embody my vulnerability. I asked Zachary if he would be willing to flog me in front of the group.

He grinned and said it would be his pleasure. I knew that being flogged would be painful and I wanted it to be. I wanted to make visible the invisible pain I constantly experienced about my belly. It seemed like a good idea, but as my turn approached I started to feel scared.

Would I be able to stay present in my body while being flogged, naked, in front of this group of men? Would I just fall back on enduring something unpleasant just to make it end? I needed help with this experiment. I asked Ken if he would look me in the eye from a couple of feet away and breathe with me while I was being flogged. I wanted his help to maintain mindful breathing so I could keep my awareness in my body—and not distract myself—until the experience ended.

When I think about it now—Zachary inflicting pain while Ken kept me in my body so that I could experience and learn from the pain—I believe that we were practicing something that was going to be my life for quite a while after Zachary's death.

The night before his death, Zachary and I had a delightful, long-lasting, highly erotic sexual experience. It was very different than other times we'd had together. Of course, in our almost fifteen years together, we'd had a lot of sex: Tantric sex, hot sex, creative sex, experimental sex, sex for hours, ho-hum sex, quickies. Until that moment, I would have said that there was not much new ground for us to cover erotically. But twenty-four hours before he died, we had sex that was perplexingly difficult to categorize.

It was not the hottest, craziest, sexiest, tamest, most connected, least connected, most intense, least intense, or wildest sex. While it was particularly sweet, hot, and connected, there was something else. It was, quite palpably, the most *different*. That is the only word I can find for it. It was not different in how we used our bodies or who put what where; it was different in the energetic exchange going on between us and within us. We didn't do anything out of the ordinary.

The next day I asked him what it had been like for him and he, like me, was aware that something about it had been very different, but he had no idea what it meant or how to describe the difference. The different quality of the encounter stuck with me. It sticks with me today.

A couple of days after he died, it hit me. The reason neither of us could come up with words to describe what was happening during our last night together was that the sexual energy exchanged that night was us saying 'goodbye' to one another. Goodbye to our shared lives and all we had known together.

My feelings were confusing. I was comforted by this awareness that his death was a part of some larger plan about which, at some level, we must have known. It was hauntingly beautiful that we had said 'goodbye' in such a potent-in-one-another's-bodies way—and it was heartbreaking.

In Tantra, there is no real distinction between God and us. We are God. This concept is one with which I struggle. If I am God, why don't I have the power to make it so that Zachary didn't die? If I am not God, then how can I explain the way that I somehow touched the Mystery—the leaks of knowledge—that foreshadowed Zachary's death? I cannot explain it.

How did all of those leaks occur? Was the time and place of his death preordained? Did he and I have some karmic agreement about what "experiment" (the experiment we chose was to be together for almost fifteen years and have a child together) we were going to do in this life and when it would end? Did he and Zoe have a similar karmic agreement? Do Zoe and I have some karmic agreement to both lose the man we loved? Did she and I choose a life path that would set us up to work through that experience together? Did Zachary and the driver of the Honda CR-V have some karmic agreement to be at that spot at that time? *I don't know.*

What if, after our negotiation about leaving for home, we'd decided to stay at the lake cabin for an extra night? Would he still be here? Would he have died in some other tragic "accidental" way at the cabin at 12:22 AM? *I don't know.*

How is it that he rushed into that fourth lane of traffic at that precise moment and not three seconds before or three seconds after? How is it that the driver was driving at forty-three miles per hour and not forty-two or forty-four? And why were the street lights out that night? Had any one of these seemingly random factors been different by a very small margin, Zachary likely would have missed that moment to die. Would he have died a few moments later, or fifty years later? *I don't know.*

I choose to assume that we were all exactly where we needed to be to learn what we needed to learn. I know that sounds weak and "spiritual-lite," but really, what other explanation is there? I cannot think of another explanation. Was this fucked-up series of random events and leaks all made up to make me feel somehow better? I am not sure that the leaks make me feel better. At times, I think a fucked-up series of random events would make me feel better or would somehow help make my grief easier or less complicated. These leaks continue to gnaw at me and make discounting the mystery of life impossible. Before and after Zachary's death, in my study of Tantra, I have learned to submit to this mystery.

*I don't know.*

Submission is trusting something vaster and wiser than myself to be in charge. I had to submit to all of the I-don't-knows. This painful yet vital aspect of my healing also releases me from the "if onlys."

Without submitting to the mystery of the leaks, Zachary's death, and the inevitability of his being in the right/wrong place at the right/wrong time, I might have gone nuts.

# CHAPTER 8

*Tantra is not sex. Sex is pigs making little pigs.*
—*Rahasya*

ONCE ZOE BEGAN school, Ken and I needed to change our meeting time to a bit earlier; he came between 4:30 and 5:00 AM to support me, love me, and hold me as I processed my grief in an embodied way. Each morning I made a pot of chai for us. We would take the teapot down to the basement, which we now called the Wailing Room, and talk for a while. I then followed my desire, which, in the beginning, meant that I cried and Ken held me and supported me through wave after wave of heartrending grief. His desire was to show up for me and to be present with me. While that hardly felt erotic in any pleasurable way, we were using our bodies, being in our bodies, to hold and move my painful, broken feelings.

One morning during a particularly intense crying jag, I writhed off the couch onto the floor. Ken followed and held me from behind—spooning me as I settled down. We laid there while he held me and I attempted to calm my breath.

Then a terrifying thing happened. I became aware of Ken's cock and balls pressed against me through our clothes.

At first, I was confused about the fact that I'd noticed this at all. Then I noticed that my awareness of his body (including his cock and balls) felt oddly comforting. *Was that okay? Was I supposed to feel any good sensations in the midst of my pain? Was I being disrespectful of Zachary? Or more accurately, was I being disrespectful to the memory of Zachary?* It had been only a handful of weeks since Zachary had died and it was beginning to sink in that he, in fact, no longer existed. He was now just a memory.

I noted this feeling of pleasure to Ken and he didn't freak out or react, really, in any way. He just held steady. As he stayed present and held steady, the anxious questions and thoughts in my head started to quiet.

During my prior year of Tantric exploration with Ken, I had begun to cultivate a curiosity about my body, pleasure, and sensation that challenged and replaced my old habit of self-judgment. As I acknowledged to myself that what I was feeling that morning was indeed pleasure, I again burst into tears.

Experiencing pleasure after writhing in pain and being flooded with tears seemed profoundly... something. Not wrong; not bad—but not altogether right, either. The subtle erotic pleasure of feeling Ken's body next to mine was... *what?* That hint of pleasure was somehow confusing. Terrifying. But it was more than that.

*It was alive.*

Feeling alive at that moment was such a contradiction to my system. I did not know what to do with a feeling that was incredibly subtle, yet powerful. So, I did what I had been doing all along. I cried.

Then (I do not remember how or why) I decided to move the subtle pleasurable sensation of Ken's cock and balls from my butt, my root chakra, up through my chakra system. I was able to coax it up beyond my cock and balls to my belly, where it stayed stuck for a bit and I felt a little sick. Eventually, I was able to move this very subtle erotic energy to my heart. I suddenly and surprisingly felt like my heart had cracked open all over again; the pain in my heart was now decidedly worse, somehow more deep and intense.

I was back to crying and writhing in pain.

After some time, minutes or more, I pulled myself together enough to wake my daughter for school and face my day. I noticed that I was actually feeling better than I had since Zachary had died. I was not feeling good, but I was feeling just a bit less bad. I was sure it was the experience of that tiny bit of aliveness in the wake of his death which allowed me to feel "better." I had not experienced anything but death in weeks. I'd been functioning as a grieving single parent of a grieving kid, and I hadn't felt alive.

*Is this a fluke? Am I capable of holding both my sadness and pain along with pleasure? Is it okay to experience an erotic moment in the wake of the death of my husband? What will my friends and family think?*

I knew if I was not able to hold these seemingly conflicting experiences of pleasure/pain, alive/dead in the container of awareness that Ken and I were creating, I ran the risk of getting lost in pleasure which could easily become addictive. I did not want to escape my pain through pleasure. Addictive pleasure is still pleasure, but I knew it would distract me from the work at hand—to heal my heart, mind, and body from the loss of the man I loved more deeply than anyone. I remembered Ken's words from sessions prior to Zachary's death: "Feel the sadness, or fear, or whatever you're feeling along with the erotic pleasure."

My work was to somehow integrate this loss into the fabric of my new life. Seeking pleasure to somehow distract me from the pain of loss would not help me to integrate my loss of him in the new life I was trying to create. *How do I feel both the pleasure and the grief?*

Running from the pain by submerging in pleasure was not the path I wanted to choose. But I'd had a glimpse into how subtle erotic pleasure, when moved up the chakra system to my heart, somehow opened my heart to a deeper, fuller, and excruciating healing experience. When I was able to experience the pain more fully, I had more openness to connect with and think about Zoe. I knew that embracing my pain was the way to heal. And this path scared the shit out of me.

I also knew that I needed to not get stuck in death. Getting stuck would be disrespectful to the memory of Zachary and neglectful of Zoe's needs. I trusted that options for my new life would emerge as I submitted to my pain. A new idea clicked in my brain: with pleasure as a life preserver, I could submerge and stay afloat. However, I also knew from my psychotherapeutic training that using pleasure to distract from the pain gives pain unconscious power and control. I did not want this to happen to me.

Allowing pleasure to coexist with pain was an intriguing experiment I wanted to explore. I recalled the night back in the temple when Ken's shirt caught fire and he first introduced the notion that both discomfort and pleasure could coexist. Neither Ken nor I ever guessed we would embrace that same practice to heal from the death of Zachary. Allowing myself to experience the subtle pleasure generated by Ken's cock and balls connecting with my butt was the beginning of embracing decidedly erotic energy to help deepen my experience of pain. It became the bedrock of both my healing from Zachary's death and my journey as a student of Tantra.

A few mornings later while in the Wailing Room, Ken asked me what I wanted. *I remember this question from Zachary's first Tantra session!* I thought about it and asked to be held as I cried and allowed myself to feel waves of fear. His clothed cock and balls touching my butt a few days earlier was an unintentional event. My slightly increased ease with the rest of my day was the data from my/our experiment not to recoil from the pleasure of his body holding mine. The pleasure principle—pleasure heals and the deeper the pleasure, the deeper the healing—was one of the bedrocks of Tantric practice.

Ken wondered aloud about our foray into this particular principle in the face of death. We did not set out to experiment with using eroticism to heal from death. We started out with Ken holding a steady presence as I cried and began the Herculean task of creating a new life in the face of unbearable loss.

"We're at a crossroads here. Do you want to continue this exploration? I've never used pleasure to heal from the loss of a loved one. Neither has my teacher."

How could I not? I had distinct memories of pleasure healing me before Zachary died, and I had the slightest whiff of healing from our accidental brush with pleasure.

*Really, what do I have to lose?*

We decided to try using pleasure as a tool to heal from my loss. Ken and I were familiar to one another; our bodies remembered our intimate connection from some months ago; and yet as we deliberately reengaged erotically, we explored like new and very frightened lovers.

We were clumsy, self-conscious, and tentative. *Do I smell okay? If I hold on, will I ever let go? Can I breathe? Can I actually give anything? Can I allow in any pleasure? Can I bring this uncomfortable, clumsy, tentative pleasure to the parts of me (my heart and my belly mostly) that are emotionally devastated? And will this help?*

This was the experiment upon which we embarked.

# CHAPTER 9

*Tantra loves, and loves unconditionally. It never says no to anything whatsoever, because everything is part of the whole, and everything has its own place in the whole, and the whole cannot exist with anything missing from it.*

—*Osho*

ZACHARY AND I signed up for a second weekend-long Tantra workshop for gay men. The focus of this weekend was on the subtle energetic body—the chakra system. I had a vague sense of what the chakra system was, but it was only a vague sense—something about energy centers in the body and certain psychological issues being linked to particular chakras. I gathered that there was some esoteric way of communicating between the chakras; my understanding was clearly murky.

Once again, we began the workshop with getting-to-know-you exercises, and much less surprising to me this time, by the end of the first evening we ended up naked. The exercises had given us some sense of who our fellow participants were and what they brought to the table in terms of their eroticism, and their psychological and personality strengths/struggles, as well as how we each related to and connected with our bodies. I was beginning to see how, from a Tantric perspective, the the relationship we have with and to our bodies is often a lens on the relationship we have with the world around us. When we are not at peace in our bodies, we have difficulty finding peace in intimate relationships, and as we navigate our daily lives. Our relationship with our bodies mirrors our relationship with the world around us.

*As within, so without.*

I had read that for men the first chakra is located just inside the anus at the root of the spine. The second chakra is located just behind and a little up from the cock and balls. The third chakra sits at the belly. The fourth is at the heart. The fifth is at the throat. The sixth is at the third-eye (just in between and a little up from the eyebrows), and the seventh chakra is at the top of the head (the "crown" chakra).

The focus of this weekend was an exploration of the first three chakras, with some instruction on how to move energy up and down through the chakra system.

I felt completely calm and prepared for a nothing-about-Tantra-will-surprise-me experience. That cockiness, a trait I am generally quite fond of about myself, demonstrated my complete inexperience with Tantra. Because everything—really, everything—is an experiment and there is always new data to be gathered.

Saturday morning began with ten men sitting naked in a circle while one of the leaders talked about the chakra system. I felt excited to have all of this knowledge distilled to an hour lecture. We so rarely learned Tantra this way, and lectures are my preferred mode of learning. This was going to be a good day. I would use my brain to learn, which is where I am most comfortable.

We learned that the first chakra, also called the root chakra, is related to instinct, security, money, and survival. Energy through the root chakra is how we ground as we connect with the earth. Much of our unconscious gunk resides in our root. The fundamental questions which energetically reside in this chakra are: "Am I okay? Will I be okay? Will I be able to get what I need?"

When blocks reside in this chakra, we often experience anxiety, money issues, and a general lack of being present in our bodies and in our lives.

"You can bet when someone is stressed about paying the rent, the first chakra is involved," explained one of the leaders. "Clumsy and accident-prone folks also tend to have blocks in their first chakra. Other life issues that can result in a root chakra block are issues around food, shelter, and other basic needs. "We are not sure if the life issues cause the energetic block or if the energetic disruption in this chakra causes the life issues." *Fascinating... The body and the mind and how we are in the world are all related.* My mind was delighted in this particular chicken and egg question. *How can I use this lens into my therapeutic work?*

For many of us, the easiest, most efficient, and most direct access to this energy center is through the anus. This is one of many reasons many of us find anal sex to be pleasurable and compelling. Anal stimulation awakens root chakra energies and can encourage these energetic 'blocks' to loosen up and start flowing with increased ease. Ken reminded us, "Energies stimulated here act as the generator or power source for our whole energetic system."

I noticed that I was clenching my butt rather tightly during this part of the lecture.

After the introduction to the root chakra, we were asked to take a moment to think about our butt's history. Had it been hurt? What makes it feel good? Who has access to it? Where do we experience ease around our butt? Do we experience ease here ever? When did we learn about pleasure and the butt, or shame, or fear? *Who knew my history with my butt was something worthy of a Tantric exploration?*

Then we each took a turn standing in the center of the circle and showing all of the other men our butts—really giving them each a look, up close and personal.

I had seen quite a few butts in my day and many, many men had seen mine. None of those experiences prepared me for the vulnerability and discomfort I experienced both when it was my turn to show my asshole to this group of open and caring men, and while I was bearing witness for them. *How do I do this? I know how to do this while being sexual, but how do I do this now? In this setting? When it is not about sex? How do I begin to own, no less share, my complex story? While naked? While purposefully and intentionally showing the most private part of my body? Just fucking breathe...*

While intensely uncomfortable, showing myself in this way was freeing. I was okay. *I am okay...I think?*

Then the exercise became more challenging. We were asked to tell our butt/asshole stories to the group. Shame, betrayal, longing, fear, pain, hemorrhoids, constipation, disappointment, fissures, pleasure, need, humiliation, want, desire, shame, and more shame. Here is where much of our real and metaphorical 'shit' resides.

These were the stories we told and witnessed. These stories became part of the weekend container we were creating. I was moved and saddened to hear how so many of us had lost access to any pleasure, control, or sense of ease around our butts.

*What would our world be like if we hadn't lost access to free flowing pleasure here? How is it possible to have lost so much access to pleasure? How is it that our stories are not filled with the wonder and indescribable pleasure of our butts and butt play?*

The room was quiet. The room was heavy with the weight of our shared pain and vulnerability. A dozen naked men were sharing literal and metaphorical glimpses of our assholes and the stories they held. My mind was racing and my heart hurt. I was not feeling the slightest bit sexy. I don't think any of us were.

So, this being Tantra, we were asked to play.

The Tantric pleasure principle is simple: there is healing power in pleasure and the deeper the pleasure the deeper the healing. Simple, right? We were asked to test our own experiences with the pleasure principle as we processed some of what we shared about our particular butt story. We broke into groups of three and took turns asking for pleasure in, around, or directed toward our butts. One person received the specific pleasure he requested while another offered the requested pleasure, and the third simply witnessed—held the container. *They are not really asking us to do this, are they? Now? Really?* We awkwardly and nervously began to give and receive pleasure with one another while we simultaneously held our individual and collective struggles with our butts. Over the nervous murmurs from around the room, I heard Ken's gentle voice, "Remember to bring awareness to your butt stories right along with pleasure you are receiving... You can hold both the struggle and the pleasure together... the deeper the pleasure, the deeper the healing." *He really means this. At least he sounds like me means this.* "Bring pleasure to the parts that hurt...the hurt is craving pleasure"

This was my first hands-on experience with the pleasure principle. We had each shared our own, and heard one another's relationship with, our butts. With that awareness front and center, we were coached to bring pleasure to this part of our bodies; to bring pleasure while simultaneously being aware of all of the history and pain we shared.

I have never been explicitly encouraged to bring pleasure to my butt. Most of us had only accidentally discovered this pleasure portal and then began the years-long process of self acceptance that came with seeking others like us.

While pleasure for pleasure's sake is a delightful way to spend time, this exercise was more directed. The experiment we were being asked to partake was to bring pleasure to a specific part of our bodies. The part of our bodies we had spent time sharing and talking about without any physical engagement. Going into this triad, we each held our own complicated feelings about our relationship with our butts while also holding parts of each man's individual painful narratives of their relationship with their butts. The challenge was to bring pleasure to another's butt while holding these complex narratives front and center.

*Who does this? Who intentionally holds his pain front and center while accessing eroticism? Alone or, more radically, with others? And how do I do this?*

I had never intentionally kept conscious of my pain while engaging in eroticism (or any other kind of pleasure). It was challenging to make room for both simultaneously.

Tears, nervous laughter, sounds of awkward repositioning, and tentative moans of pleasure filled the room. *Where am I? What am I doing? How is this even possible?* Things were clicking - bringing pleasure to the parts of our bodies where we held shame, pain, and fear, and then collecting the data from that 'experiment.' *What am I going to discover here?* Smiling, I looked around the room seeing men's butts in all sorts of positions - the scene warms my heart. We were all clumsily bringing various amounts of pleasure to an ever-present, seldom discussed, complicated part of our erotic pleasure centers.

This exercise was one of my first experiences of the freedom we gain by practicing Tantra (Ken talked about freedom on the first night we spoke of Tantra and has always reminded us that that was the purpose of practicing Tantra). I suspected the other workshop participants were experiencing a glimpse of freedom as well; the energy in the room was palpably more relaxed, alive and light.

People were no longer stuck in their isolation, pain, or shame. Owning our individual and collective stories, while giving and receiving pleasure on our own terms, allowed us to reconnect ourselves to our butts and access our own pleasure in a more grounded and intentional manner. And as we were incrementally able to do that, the collective energy of our group was more light-hearted and alive.

The healing power of pleasure. *Really? It works? Bringing pleasure precisely where it hurts? How the fuck? Gathering the data?* I was intrigued how asking someone to rim me for all of three minutes could bring me enough pleasure to soothe the discomfort I had felt after sharing my story. I was moved by how merely lightly and lovingly touching my person's butt brought him to tears of joy and gratitude. "Your touch on my ass somehow short-circuited my self-hatred and my shame about who I am." I was deeply grateful. We both thanked our third person for witnessing our erotic engagement.

Most people (regardless of orientation) learn about the pleasures of butt play furtively, often alone or in the dark in a way that fosters shame. This normal, delightful and curious exploration is invisible to most of us until we consciously seek it out.

After what seemed like an eternity of butts, first chakra talk, play, tears, etc., we took a much needed break. We ate snacks, drank tea, stepped outside, and talked about nothing in particular - just a group of mostly naked men getting to know one another.

The erotic pleasures given and received during this exercise stayed with me long after the sexual play had ended— even days and weeks later. I had a new awareness of my butt. I was able to feel its energy, and with that awareness I had choices. I could choose to clench or relax—a simple freedom.

Next, we repeated the exercise with our second chakra, which is slightly above and behind the cock and balls. The fundamental questions of this chakra are, What do I desire? What do I feel? What am I going to create? Will I create off-spring, a garden, community, art? Can I own my desire—my sexual desire as well as all of my other creative desires?

"We literally create life from this chakra," Ken explained, "You can imagine what some conscious awareness here could bring to your creative lives. Imagine the power you could harness if you bring awareness to and begin to harness the the creative energies of this chakra.

"Conversely, when there are blocks in the second chakra, you will often experiences impotence, premature ejaculation, difficulty in achieving orgasm, and compulsive or addictive sexual behaviors."

My mind raced as to how I could use this lens in my psychotherapy practice when men came in with these particular sexual challenges. *How do they relate to their own sense of ownership of the life they want to create? What do they want to create? What might get in the way for them? For whom are they creating? What are they afraid to create? And on and on...* Sexual dysfunction literature doesn't exactly look at these issues from the underlying perspective of "second chakra energies." *No wonder we are not particularly good at treating these issues.*

Then it was back to the center of the circle, and one by one, each of us showed the group our cock and balls. I had seen many cock and ball sets in my day, most often in highly sexual arenas. My experience with men's cocks was that I got to play with them in ways I found pleasurable, and I assumed they found pleasurable. Here, I was being taken on an intimate and up-close tour of eleven wildly varied cocks and balls and all of their history and experiences. While I find cocks and balls extremely hot, this experience was not remotely arousing. It was sacred; sacred taps into something greater than self, greater than the conscious ego.

One of the principles of this lineage involves "tapas" and "spanda" Basically this is a practice (or 'trick' as I like to call it) we can use to learn more about how we tick; in other words, it is a practice which can raise awareness around something familiar or habitual we do which allows a new awareness or understanding to emerge.

I was not engaging in my usual habit of sex around men's cocks; I was suspending the habit (tapas) of sexualizing these beautiful cocks, and in doing so, I learned something greater, more awesome, about these men and their cocks (spanda). What showed up for me was something akin to grace or the divine. We each shared our cocks and balls in such a way that our hearts opened, as something like love was present.

Having the courage to display ourselves, to invite one another's curious or hungry gaze to our crotches, felt radical. Sacred. The courage to directly take in and savor another man's cock and balls and not avert ones eyes was also radical. I was experiencing a bigger truth, and together the group was creating a kind of magic energy with our honesty and courage and our cock and balls.

I wasn't the only one who felt this gift of openness and appreciation. While we all came across as some combination of proud, tentative, ashamed, giggly, and scared while showing our cocks, we were all exquisitely reverent. My first chakra was activated from the pleasure I just received at my butt, and I felt a low-key, easy erotic energy stirring. "The root chakra energy, which is deeply grounding, sets a sturdy foundation for deeper second chakra pleasure" I overheard Ken telling a bewildered participant. *Now it starts to make sense...*

I felt present and open to the group, and for the first time, I felt what Ken meant when he said that this energy was the generator of life—my creative life force. It was like discovering a gift I'd always possessed, but never before recognized as a gift.

Next up we each took a turn showing ourselves, we took turns telling the biographies of our cocks and balls. For being such sacred parts of our bodies, most of our cock and ball stories were pretty checkered—abuse, desire met, desire denied, shame, grief, botched circumcisions, STIs, longing, cumming too fast, cumming too slowly, not cumming at all, fun, ease, betrayal, not big enough, not good enough, not big enough, more longing, not good enough, not fat enough, not big enough. It was a lot for which to stay present.

Surprisingly (or maybe not), even the more well-endowed guys had the same insecurities about their cocks. All of this conflicted and jagged energy was present in our circle.

Once again we broke-out into triads with the direction of asking for and offering pleasure to our second chakras via pleasure to our cocks and balls. "Remember to hold your and others' challenging cock and ball histories while you are both giving and receiving pleasure... This is how we can experiment with the pleasure principle..." Ken's voice caught my ear over the nervous murmurs of our triads

Even though I noticed a shift had occurred with our individual and collective energies after engaging in first chakra pleasure, I noticed that the group seemed tentative about engaging in second-chakra pleasure after telling stories about our cocks and balls. *Wait. What? A groups of (naked) gay men hesitant about offering and receiving pleasure to our cock and balls? This can't be...*

I still felt befuddled and self conscious asking for and giving erotic pleasure around emotional and psychic pain - and to ask for it specifically while a third member of our group just lovingly held the space while bearing witness to the whole exchange. I was good at talking about emotional pain and helping clients heal through loving talk. I realized that I was experiencing the influence of Puritanism on my notions about the healing potential of sexual play. In that weekend workshop, I hit my resistance to what would later save my life: bringing pleasure, erotic pleasure, to parts of myself that felt emotionally broken, and doing so out in the open.

Eventually, we each gave and received pleasure at and around our second chakras. The heaviness in the room lifted for the second time that day. Because we went into the experience with a shared awareness of our stories, we were able to be more present while offering and receiving pleasure. We didn't have to pretend to be other than who we were. We did not have to pretend to be more sexy than we were at that moment. Because our stories were on the table, and welcomed, they no longer had to be exiled from our erotic selves. We wove our stories in with the eroticism.

*How is it that I do not have the faintest idea how to pleasure these cocks? How is it that I seemingly have no idea what would feel good to me? Stop. Just breathe. Just breathe. That stupid 'what do you want?' question again.*

We began this exercise with the same clumsily moving bodies and nervous laugher as we began the last one. Quickly the room quieted as we all settled in to our chosen roles of pleasure seeker, giver or observer. In a bit, quiet moans of pleasure and muted laughter filled the room. We were allowing those parts of ourselves which we find unacceptable, insufficient, embarrassing or shameful to be (often) literally touched by another in a pleasurable way. Pleasurable touch in the way we specifically asked for it. "Bring pleasure to where it hurts... use the pleasure to enhance your experience of your pain... your shame... Don't forget to collect the data... Are you asking for what you want? Are you getting what you want?" Ken's voice weaving in and out of my awareness.

During our post-triad debrief the data was consistent for all of us: we found that pleasure did not mask the intensity of our stories, but instead, somehow, pleasure simultaneously amplified and eased our pain. Our cock and ball histories felt less powerful.

We reconvened and were led in a meditation trying to differentiate the pleasure we had received at our first chakra from the pleasure we received at our second chakra. This level of discernment of where my pleasure resided in me was new. I knew and had experience with the different pleasures of, say, fucking someone and being fucked by someone. But I had never thought about relating these pleasures to energy centers in my body—or using those energy centers to work on different psychological issues that plagued me. Pleasure is far more nuanced than I had been aware.

The distinction of the subtle and not-so-subtle pleasures and energies at the different chakras was intriguing. In the workshop, we used gross (obvious) erotic energies, (like when I both rimmed and was rimmed in a room while others were giving various pleasures to other butts), to open us to experience energies which were more subtle in nature. The greater ease I experienced after the rimming was more memorable than the rimming itself. The post-rimming ease was subtle in comparison to the actual rimming yet more powerfully long lasting. Ken often said that the subtle pleasures of Tantra are by far the most potent; his words were finally making sense.

Ken teaches that in Tantra all energy is vibrational. Quantum physicists say the same. During and after an erotic experience, the vibration of our physical selves is altered. After being rimmed, I had a physical awareness of my butt and an energetic awareness of the new vibration that was running through it. The feeling is hard to describe; you really have to experience it. I learned to start by listening and feeling for it in my physical body and in, what Ken refers to, my subtle energetic body. The experience was confusing my mind, but starting to make some sense in my body. Meditating on the differences in the pleasures of first and second chakras started to open the door to understanding pleasure differently, mostly because I could locate different pleasure centers in my body. What happened after the obvious hands-on pleasuring of my butt was quite subtle and lasted for weeks —and historically I did not pay attention to the subtle.

Then came the most challenging work of the day for me. We moved on to the third chakra, the belly—where issues of power and control, and domination and submission, reside. The fundamental questions of this chakra are: Can I be all of who I am in the world and have it work out well? Am I willing to submit to the entirety of who I am and not just to what others think I should be? Am I willing to submit not just to who I think I should be, but to who I truly am?

Ken explained that the belly chakra embodies our will, our "gut" knowing—our personal power. When we have blocks at the belly chakra, we often experience a fear of vulnerability. You can look good, but not feel good. Rigidity at this chakra comes from not breathing in a deep and relaxed way, reflecting a deep fear of being seen. Can I breathe in a relaxed way and be who I am?

*Do I ever breathe in a relaxed way? Am I ever okay with being who I am?*

I have what I consider to be garden-variety insecurities about my butt, and cock and balls. Yet my thoughts, feelings, and reactions to my belly are quite distorted. I am a solid, strong, thickly built Middle Eastern man, but cannot see myself in that light. I vacillate between thinking I look acceptable to unsightly to obese. That switch can happen in fifteen minutes or fifteen seconds. So it was with some trepidation that I stood up when it was my turn and gave my fellow Tantric explorers a tour of my belly—from all angles, without sucking it in, while breathing. Sporadically breathing.

*Not so fun. I am studying Tantra why?*

Each of the other men in the group did the same. And to my body's surprise (I think I had some intellectual sense of this) even the flat-bellied men had issues, insecurities, and distortions similar to mine. Even Zachary, who had a flat, muscular, hairy-in-all-the-right-places belly, felt uneasy about that part of his body. Shame, vulnerability, judgment, and self-loathing seemed to sit in all of our bellies. We all struggled with not sucking it in. We all struggled with relaxedly breathing.

For a moment, I was able to step out of my own distorted self-image to feel the group's collective pain around our bodies, desirability, and self-hatred. I always feel more centered and connected when I can step out of my own world to feel compassion for what others are experiencing.

After the belly tour and narrative, we moved on to pleasure. We gathered in triads once again with the same instruction: bring pleasure to this chakra-specifically while holding our individual and collective belly stories right along with the pleasure. I was completely befuddled about how to bring pleasure to my belly. It seemed... something... *Maybe wrong? Paradoxical? Enigmatic?*

First, none of us had any idea where the belly chakra resides. Our first task was to ask our partners to explore our bellies to find that sweet spot that was the energetic center of the third chakra. This spot sits differently in all of us. So, with gentle, once again awkward, and clumsy prodding with his hand, fist, and chin, my partner put various amounts of pressure on different regions of my belly until he hit a spot that felt unlike the others. *Found it!*

When he placed firm pressure on my newly discovered energetic spot that was my belly chakra, I felt deep pleasure mixed with a delightful, confusing, and unfamiliar pain. The first time Ken had worked on my belly, the pain was not all pleasurable. This time, the pain had new and interesting good feelings mixed with pain. *It hurts so good!* After that experience, my breathing felt easier.

The hands-on exercises, or as I was learning to say, "experiments," focused on the belly were differently pleasurable than the others. I never knew I had an energy center in my belly that could be physically stimulated by another person. I had not experienced that particular mix of pain and pleasure before. And most certainly not in that region of my body.

Since that day I have been more at peace with my belly than I had been in forty years. Ken's words echoed again in my head, "It's the subtle energies where Tantra comes alive." Bringing pleasure to the very part of my body I had walled off from pleasure for most of my life subtly changed my relationship to my belly. *The healing power of pleasure? Radical. Fucking radical.*

That weekend we did not have a chance to explore the fourth, fifth, sixth, and seventh chakras with any depth. However, we did do a culmination of our explorations of the first, second, and third chakras by intentionally practicing moving energy up and down the chakra system. I was excited. This was what I thought Tantra was all about and what would lead to those four-hour orgasms.

We worked in pairs; luckily for me, the man with whom I was paired was energetically, erotically, and emotionally a good fit. Our assignment was to take turns generating first and second chakra energy. Phil used his finger to tease my asshole, gently massaging my sphincter and then pushed in some, but stopping, leaving me wanting more. He did this a few more times before he used his other hand to coax my soft cock to be hard. I physically and mentally got it: he'd helped me make an energetic connection between my first and second chakras. I was one of those guys who remained soft while getting fucked and was not in touch with my first chakra when I was hard and receiving attention on my cock. These two energetic centers had never before communicated; when one was on, the other was decidedly off. At this moment, both were on. I was intrigued.

I kept trying to "see" the connection between the two chakras in my mind's eye so I could figure out how they were working in my body. My partner helped my body experience this connection using his hands, mouth, and fingers.

Once the energy from my first chakra arrived at my second chakra, my cock was alive and activated. He then worked my cock and balls to get more energy going, and once I was ready, we moved that energy to my belly. He used his hands to make the actual physical connection between my cock and balls and my belly by repeatedly moving his hands from the base of my hard cock up to my belly.

Without Phil physically guiding me by moving his hands upward from the base of my cock up to my belly, I am certain I would have been lost as to what to do. I suspect I would have fallen back on my familiar habit of enjoying the sexual energy in and around my cock and balls. But as he continued to guide the energy to my belly physically, I began to feel something move internally. I actually felt warmth and a sense of ease in my belly as the energy flowed into the third chakra. Then he worked my belly while I allowed his hand to guide me, pulling the energy up from my butt and cock.

When Phil moved his hands repeatedly from my belly to my heart all of a sudden–bam!, I felt what I can only describe as a physically open heart suffused with a feeling of love. My heart chakra was activated, but not because I loved Phil (I hardly knew him) but because I was able to move the erotic first and second chakra energies up to my heart. It was a spacious state of being through which I was experiencing him, the room around me, and the whole world. The feeling was big, and it wasn't taking place as a thought in my head—my body was inhabiting the experience.

I was able to move energy to my throat chakra, third-eye, and finally my crown. With Phil's hands-on help, I was able to bring the energy back down to ground at my root chakra. While I did not experience this as a whole-body orgasm, I was excited that I actually did it! I had learned a new, seemingly technical skill.

This moving energy thing was something I'd been aware of for twenty years, but I'd always thought I would need to be inside a woman to make it happen. It happened with Phil, who was definitely not a woman. Moving energy was about accessing my own eroticism.

Moving erotic energy did not come easily to me the next time I tried—or the time after that. But, as with most of Tantra, I accept that it is a practice—not unlike meditation, movement, nutrition, and breathing. So practice I did, and still do.

# CHAPTER 10

*Put away your pointless taboos and restrictions on sexual energy—rather help others to truly understand its wonder, and to channel it properly.*

—God,

*Channeled by Neal Donald Walsh*

SINCE ZACHARY AND I had first begun doing Tantric work with Ken, we had dramatically altered our relationship container. We were both engaging with people we knew who lived in town, and we were having an intimate ongoing relationship with Ken independent of each other.

Tampering with our long-successful arrangement made me anxious, although it seemed an easy change for Zachary. Ken suggested we see this change in our container as an "experiment" to which we would bring our awareness. *Of course he did! That is what he always says! He always does go back to the principles when he is a little lost.* He also challenged us not only to collect data from the experiment during our sexual encounters, but also to collect data in the hours, days, weeks, and months following each encounter. *I get it... I get it... Everything is an experiment...And if everything is an experiment, that means that there is no prescribed right or wrong way to be in the world. Ahhhh, viewing everyone as*

*an experiment gives us freedom to explore uncharted waters.
And, don't forget to collect the data...*

Because we were with a third, more experienced, person,
Zachary and I tried some new behaviors that Ken thought we
might find interesting. Some were fun, some were super fun,
and some were downright life-altering.

Tantric practitioners in this lineage engage in this way
(including taboo) as a way of identifying with none of it.
Engaging with all that is is one of many paths to God. Bud-
dhists forsake and engage with nothing; they practice non-at-
tachment, as a way to God. The goal of most spiritual practices
is engagement with God, with many paths to this end. In our
case, our paths include engaging in activities that were traditionally seen as taboo, or kinky. Our kinky behaviors release
potential energy inherent in the specific behavior. The goal of
releasing potential energy is to add more juice to our erotic
and non-erotic life. For me, this practice also directly enhanced
the intensity and volume of energy generated in my first and
second chakras.

Before studying Tantra, I had, what I assumed to be, a
pretty typical relationship with cum in general and with mine
in particular. I associated cum with orgasm, and therefore
cum was always a welcome addition to my sexual play. Like
many gay men who came of age during the late 1980s, I also
learned to be afraid of other men's cum. Cum became associated with AIDS, which decimated and terrorized the gay
community. In addition to being, at that time, a fatal illness,
AIDS brought into laser-sharp focus our collective shame and
fear—or at least gave a laser-sharp focus to my own shame and
fear. AIDS gave the broader population an excuse to further
isolate, mistreat, and scapegoat gay men for their own sexual
shame, guilt, and confusion.

It was not surprising, then, that I became afraid of cum. It wasn't just me. Many of my gay friends and lovers had become afraid of it, too. Far too many had become afraid of sex and even closeness; some managed their fear by denying themselves sex and love. I just kept others' cum away from me, and in the process forgot how much I relished the cum of others.

Shortly after the first night that Zachary and I had first gone to the bar to meet Ken, the three of us enjoyed our first three-way sexual encounter together. Weeks later, Zachary and I started studying with Ken. After a few months of study, we decided to have another three-way Tantric sexual experience together.

Ken suggested that we play with the tapas/spanda principle of Tantra; we agreed to play in a highly sexual way and "apply tapas" (to our normal habit of cumming at the culmination of sexual play) and not cum. And, of course, to collect the data from the experiment. "Try this practice without judgment to see if you learn anything about who you are and what you want. If we can create a kind of curious container for this new experience, something new will emerge. What emerges is called spanda." He explained that in Tantra, "Spanda can be a new feeling, insight, awareness, or challenge. But, trust me, if we suspend our usual behavior of cumming, new things will emerge."

Zachary pretended to be grumpy about it, but we agreed to apply tapas to our habit of cumming at the end of this sexual encounter.

We agreed to have sex in a way that was not usual for us. *Did Zachary and I ever have sex without cumming? I don't think so.*

Being sexual without focusing on getting to the big orgasm at the end was surprisingly easy, albeit unintuitive and a touch distracting. Intellectually, not cumming did not make sense; virtually every time I had sex, I came. But we were applying tapas and waiting—waiting to see what new energies, thoughts, desires, ideas, and insights emerge. The sex lasted for hours. At the end, Zachary and I felt high in that same way we did the night we made out with Ken at the bar.

As we slowly wound down our play, the three of us headed toward the shower. In the shower, however, we were distracted by more erotic play. Given that neither of us experienced the common sharp drop in both desire for and interest in sex that follows orgasm (this is my first data point!), getting distracted by more play was easy. Ken invited us to play with pee in a sacred way. I was nervous—my usual response to new things. Zachary was excited—his usual reaction.

Ken was excited, open, and able to hold space for this thrilling, nervous, new experience. Once again, we were each in character.

Over the years, I had heard of and talked about water sports with Zachary, friends, and with clients but I had never dabbled in it. It never interested me. In fact, I had the common negative judgment about such play. For me, peeing was not sexy. Other than the pleasure of releasing my bladder when it was particularly full, I didn't experience anything akin to pleasure from urinating nor did I think much about my pee.

One of the hallmarks of conscious sex with people who are also committed to conscious sex is that one's nervousness (in my case) or excitement (in Zachary's case) was not a solo internal experience; it could be out in the open and part of the erotic experience. My anxiety—which out of the context of sexual play, was not at all sexy—was woven in to our eroticism. That alone was pretty mind-altering for me—kinky even.

As was Ken's way, he allowed Zachary and me to engage with our pee in any way that felt good or interesting to each of us... and we did.

In my previous, limited, uneducated, uninformed, and inexperienced understanding of water sports, humiliation and degradation was a part of the energetic landscape, and I was not interested in humiliation or degradation. But a larger question emerged for me: Who would want to engage with my pee? That said, what I think I know about things that I have not yet experienced in my body is usually wrong—dead wrong.

Ken got into the shower and on his knees. He invited me in with him and tentatively took my cock in his mouth. He was waiting to see if this was okay with me. It was. His eyes made it clear to me he wanted me to release my bladder while in his mouth. I tried. I could not. All the while Zachary was watching and obviously turned on.

*Breathe. Just breathe.*

Zachary offered to help; or at least to get in closer to what was happening. With Zachary behind me, arms around me, Ken took my cock into his mouth again. I was intrigued way more than I was aroused. *Everything is an experiment, right?*

After a few false starts (peeing into someone's mouth was not as easy as it might seem) I gave Ken some of my pee, and he swallowed it. As the pee was leaving my body I was surprised because I was not expecting the wave of pleasure that accompanied this gift to Ken. It felt like I was ejaculating cum. I pee for a lot longer than I cum, so the incredibly intense pleasure lasted quite a long time. I assume this had something to do with the potential energy of pee, as physiologically, orgasmic pleasure from urinating does not make sense to me, in that the mechanisms of urination (with a soft cock) and cumming (presumably with a hard cock) are quite different.

When I was finished emptying my bladder, I felt the pleasure shift. Heat was generated, and seemingly without effort or awareness, the erotic pleasure of my cock in his mouth had, in fact, moved up to my heart. I felt my heart warm and metaphorically open up in the aftermath of Ken taking my pee. I felt loved in a deep, surprisingly un-sexual way. My face and head tingled as my crown chakra opened. I felt quite high, as though I had smoked high-quality cannabis.

At the time, I had no idea of the magnitude of what had just happened. It took me the better part of a year to unpack and integrate what was the beginning of a fun, powerful, and sexy habit. As I studied more, however, I realized what I had experienced that first day of pee play—feeding someone pee immediately brought erotic energy up the chakras of my subtle energy system.

As I experienced the pleasure of my energy moving up and energizing my chakra system, my crown chakra opened. Once that happened, the energy traveled down my energetic system deeply grounding me. Once the energy settled in to my root chakra, my mind quieted, and a sense of well being came over me. What I felt in that moment was intense pleasure and a feeling (in my heart!) of being loved. I was calm, relaxed, and grounded. *A whole-body orgasm! It happened! And I wasn't even trying.*

This experience was my first of intense sexual play calming and quieting my mind. *Spanda.*

And I had not cum. *Tapas.*

Ken later explained that receiving pee is a sacrament—an outward and visible sign of inward and spiritual divine grace. His taking in my pee brought his energy to ground as quickly and profoundly as my energy went up. Ken's grounding was seemingly as pleasurable for him as my opening was for me. Once his energy went to ground, it moved up his internal system and he, too, experienced his energetic system being charged with pleasure culminating in his crown chakra opening.

Zachary was still watching with a sly, curious grin and hard-on to match. Next was his turn. Zachary and I switched places, and he gave Ken his cock and Ken received Zachary's pee.

Zachary's face relaxed as it flushed with pleasure. He too was experiencing orgasm in a new way.

We had experienced the external marriage of yin and yang. We had been able to exchange these energies and feel each other's experience. And then, in each of our separate bodies, connected through cock and mouth, we were able to do what is considered a foundation stone of Tantra: we allowed an internal marriage of yin (which moves up the energetic system) and yang energy (which moves down the energetic system), resulting in whole-body erotic pleasure, greater consciousness, and quieter minds.

Anecdotal reports from mostly heterosexuals who engage in drinking their partner's pee are that each partner experiences a degree of intimacy and connection not otherwise available to them. Something about the potential energy locked up in this particular fluid, coupled with both the taboo nature and cultural repulsion surrounding urine, opens couples who regularly partake to connect, exchange energy, and enjoy deeper intimacy.

*Kink releases potential energy. How did I miss this for so long?*

That I felt love (which is how I experienced the physically warm feeling in my heart), however, was surprising and perplexing to me. Being loved is about being seen, understood, and accepted. In some way, by savoring my pee Ken allowed me to feel completely taken in and accepted. If someone wanted to take my pee (not only take it but actually be fed in the most nourishing, nurturing way) then what would he not take from me? If someone wanted that part of me, then was there anything that was wrong or bad about me? If my "waste" could be used as a tool of pleasure, then the rest of me had to be good enough too.

*Profound. Radical. Fucking Radical.*

This type of not romantic, oddly not personal, love is in the presence of God—of God's love if you will. It was not about Ken, the person—it was about Ken, the priest. He was a vehicle for me to experience God; our energy exchange allowed me to experience God's love. In that external/internal marriage, I was Ken's vehicle to experience God. That day, I became a priest to him as well.

Urination is the body ridding itself of waste. While urine is what one's body no longer needs, mere byproducts of metabolic processes, urine is sterile and not dirty (although it is treated in our society as though it is quite toxic). So how could this substance be linked with, even integral to, another's pleasure?

An alchemical process happened for Ken as he took in and energetically processed the pee and released its potential energy. He transformed what was essentially waste into something inherently and profoundly nourishing. As that internal alchemical transformation happened, I (the giver) was opened to experience transformation too—as within, so without.

This experiment was my first with eroticizing urination. With repeated practice, the data, while always nuanced, is fairly predictable. When I feed a man my pee, I feel completely full, open, loved and transformed. When he partakes of my pee, he feels full, open, warm, loved and transformed. I believe the love that we each feel is the love of God—it is clearly not about the person with whom I am exchanging this sacred fluid/energy. I sometimes have no idea who he is and have no idea what brings him to his knees desiring pee.

Also I rarely know what brings anyone to church, synagogue, temple, mosque, meditation circle, yoga class, the woods, or the baths, seeking God. I trust we all find God in ways that make sense to us. I found my path to God through my powerful sexual and sensual nature.

Giving and receiving pee is just one ritual to engage this internal marriage of yin and yang so fundamental to Tantra. This ritual was the first where I actually felt the internal marriage. It was my first opening to a whole body orgasm and something palpably bigger than me—to God.

So the heart chakra opening (or feeling of intense physical love) I experienced with Ken the first time he took my pee was not about being in love with him. At that time, I did not know Ken well. The openness I was feeling was about me and my relationship with God—not about Ken. He did not objectively know me any more before this exchange than after.

He did not objectively love me, Ed Swaya, the person, any more after than before.

*Except... maybe he did.*

Sharing the presence of God with someone does open the door to a powerful person-to-person bond. I also know that while neither Zachary nor I consumed one another's pee that day (or ever) being there while each of us had that profound experience connecting with Ken, and the equally profound experience of connecting with God, brought us closer. Without a doubt, we both experienced this closeness.

As individuals, Zachary and I used pleasure to experience the presence of God. Together Zachary and I used pleasure, kinky pleasure, to move closer to each other. This particular pleasure was new to us, and it was that newness that allowed a new opening to emerge. *Spanda.*

Although I did not know it then, this particular kink would turn out to be integral to my healing.

Applying tapas to the habit of cumming opened a new avenue of exploration (spanda) and new understanding about the nature of cum, cumming, and orgasm. Spanda is not always pleasant or pleasurable, I discovered, but when something new happens, I learn about myself which allows me more freedom. As I collected the data from a number of experiments focused on cumming or not cumming during erotic play, I could then choose what experience I wanted in any given erotic encounter.

As Ken reminded us, " If we have to cum every time we have sex, we have less freedom than when we can decide yes or no. Remember, the point of Tantra is to experience freedom."

Even though he'd had a great time, Zachary was still skeptical. Privately he told me, "That was a lot of work!"

From then on, the energetic field around my cumming (and trying to get my partner to cum) changed. Cumming was no longer something I did all of the time. When I did—and I came often—it was delightful, but delightful in a different way. I was more aware that I was choosing that destination. Choice feels good.

When I'm having sex with someone now, I'm not interested in cumming if my partner isn't interested in physically and energetically receiving my cum in his body. Cumming with spiritual intention is intoxicating for me; when my partner isn't interested, then I'd much rather have the buzz of not cumming, which is also delightful.

I've started to understand that men who love to take in cum don't just like the flavor or smell, but the energy. Both Zachary and I both were able to access that energy when we increased our consciousness around cum and cumming. We were intentional when we came, while previously we had not been. We were intentional where, how and when we gave and received cum. We had fun experimenting during our relationship with our own and each other's cum. One afternoon, we went to a bathhouse and decided to play and not cum. It was very hard to know when to stop and go home—we didn't know when we were done! That was a fun dilemma.

I have learned that the energy of cum, the importance of cum, and my experience of cum, was dependent on the context of the erotic engagement. For instance, when I jack-off, cum on my belly, and jump in the shower, my cum releases very little of its potential energy. When I give a stranger my cum after a quickie blow-job, a bit more of its inherent potential energy is released (although this depends upon the receiver's consciousness, intention, and experiences with cum). When Zachary and I played for hours and intentionally offered cum, inside each other, a magnitude of potential energy was released. With Zachary, the more intentional we were about exchanging cum, the more apparent cum's numinous qualities became.

# CHAPTER 11

*It's time we saw sex as the truly sacred art that it is. A deep meditation a holy communion and a dance with the force of creation.*

—Marcus Allen

DURING MY YEARS of stunted flirting with Tantra (before I became Ken's student), I was drawn to the idea of erotic ritual. The idea of some sort of structured eroticism as prayer or meditation appealed to me. When I later found my path into Tantra as a gay man, the question of what constitutes a ritual emerged again. I learned from Ken that at its most fundamental level, a ritual is a conscious experiment—nothing more.

While other traditions sometimes engage with the erotic in ritual, Tantric ritual often engages the erotic as a way of generating power and energy in the container created by and for the ritual.

What Ken and I were doing every morning in the Wailing Room was a Tantric ritual, but we didn't realize that—at least not right away. We were following desire, but unconsciously our practices started to take on a ritual form and shape.

For the first few weeks after Zachary died, I was a mess. All I could do was sob while Ken held me and let me fall apart.

As the months marched on and I began to feel slightly more centered, I was able to meditate a little. Ken and I would disrobe for meditation, and afterward, we would follow our desire and engage in conscious experiments to see how we could use erotic energy to bring healing to my broken heart. We moved from him simply holding me while I sobbed to generating low-key erotic energy. I noticed it, experienced it as pleasure, and then moved the subtle pleasurable energy to the parts of me that hurt. When pleasure reached my broken parts, my experience of pain increased dramatically. I felt like pleasure was cracking open the pain (lancing the boil) and in the process, cleansing the wound. The lancing always hurt and scared me. *Will it stop? Can I contain the pain? Can I bear the pain? Will I die from it? Will it stop?* Moving the energy didn't make the pain go away, it made me feel less stuck. I had a fear that if the energy got stuck in my body, I would be lost. Time and again after I brought pleasure to the hurt (which was becoming a well-traveled pathway), I found myself noticeably clearer, more awake and alive.

Grief feels like being dead inside. The world felt flat and two-dimensional, slightly surreal. The exception was when I was sharing conversation with Ken, as erotic energy circulated through my body. This circulation helped propel me through those days feeling a bit more alive, yet still terribly sad.

While being awake and alive was painful and counter-intuitive, it was remarkably effective. I was able to stay present and show up for my rather challenging life day-in and day-out. I could attend to paying bills, making lunches, packing up Zachary's stuff, sorting out our fifteen years of life together, watering the plants, and going to the grocery store. I was immensely grateful to have achieved this level of functioning. I needed to attend to my life and my grieving daughter's needs and processes. I also had to get her to and from school, keep her bathed and fed, and help keep her connected to her community.

I was not depressed for the most part, but I was grieving. Depression feels dead, while grief is brutally and painfully alive. My grief took the form of sadness, fear, and a bewildering sense of feeling lost. Paying bills or making lunches or cleaning the bathroom often felt Herculean.

One morning in the Wailing Room I was getting lost in my grief and starting to spiral into mental panic about all the decisions I needed to make and things I needed to do. My mind was racing, and Ken noticed the shift in my energy. He was holding me on the couch and scooted down between my legs.

We were already naked, and so he took my cock in his mouth and just held it there. It was a very gentle and easy pleasure to feel my soft cock in his mouth. I started to feel more present in my body. After some time, as I returned more to my body, I was slightly alarmed when I got hard. As was Ken's way, he stayed steady, with my growing cock in his mouth. Slowly, tentatively, but with great presence, he started to move his mouth and head, increasing the sensation to my cock.

My body responded in kind. *A blow job? Now?* The sensation built and expanded into my body and became intensely pleasurable, but pleasurable in the way my first black-and-blue erection after my broken pelvis was pleasurable. It hurt, and it felt good. It hurt and felt deliciously and terrifyingly alive.

While I regularly meditate, I often feel that I am not very good at it. My mind rarely quiets to the level I want or expect. My meditation is often a focus on quieting the useless (and sometimes useful) chatter. Occasionally I get a spacious moment or two of quiet. But I keep meditating, assuming it improves my life.

While Ken went down on me, I used my meditation skills to focus and be present with my cock in his mouth and throat. That level of trained conscious focus alone increases sexual pleasure. After some time, I came deep in his throat.

As we were exchanging all the pleasure a good blow-job affords, I was aware again that I was engaging in a taboo method of healing. As much as I had wondered during the erotic healing sessions I had with Ken before Zachary's death, a part of me was now wondering about the sacredness of fucking for emotional health. I was wondering if it was okay—if it would work. I had some experience using sex to heal emotional wounds; using sex to heal from grief stretched my comfort zone.

*I know it works. Why do I still wonder? Fucking Puritans!*

I wondered if I was being respectful to the memory of Zachary. I wondered if I could be a part of my community. I wondered if I was just avoiding the inevitable pain of authentically dealing with my loss., Yet I knew from how much that ejaculation hurt that I was clearly not avoiding anything.

*Fucking to heal from death? Fucking to stay alive?*

Many spiritual traditions eschew all things material and of the flesh as a path to experiencing God. In the Tantric lineage that Ken was teaching, we consciously engage with many erotic taboos in a hands-on way, with our bodies, in a sacred manner. What we were doing in the Wailing Room was engaging the taboo of intense eroticism in the service of healing from death. While we were pursuing a well-worn path (being sexual with one another), it was a new experiment for each of us. Neither Ken nor his teacher had engaged with sex as a way to heal from intense grief. I accepted that this practice was helping me, and I decided to continue with the experiment.

On this first foray into what would become intense eroticism, I came deep in his throat.

The ejaculation hurt. My cum burned as it left my body. The mix of the pleasure of the orgasm and the pain of the ejaculation was startling. I was then surprised by how my mind immediately quieted and a sense of calm and well-being came over me.

Ken grimaced. My cum tasted strong, bitter, and not pleasant. It had been made in my body while I was filled with the energy of pain, fear, brokenness, and sorrow, and I believe it literally carried those energies.

Later he told me it had a toxic quality, and he almost gagged. His first reaction was panic: he knew he had to get rid of the cum or somehow transform it so that it wouldn't harm him. As someone who is versed in both blow jobs and Tantric alchemy, he took my pain infused cum and energetically transformed it into something his body could digest and process. After he swallowed, he sent the energy to the ground so he would not be left with my pain lingering in his body.

Now both of our minds was completely quiet.

Once the burning sensation of my ejaculation passed, I experienced a calm body and a still, peaceful mind. My peaceful, chatter-free mind startled me. The calm in my body felt foreign. The stillness I experienced felt like an oasis in the middle of a desert. All I could do at that moment was to experience the peace. For a moment, my Universe made sense—not as in "this is all good," but made sense in that my beloved was dead and here I was alive, broken-hearted, well enough, and participating in our imperfect world. I had the clear sense that I was okay. Not that I was going to be okay, or that someday my life I would be okay, but in that moment of quiet, I was okay—deeply and profoundly okay.

I felt not one iota of denial of Zachary's death or of how much it fucking hurt. It was okay. I was okay. Neither the calm nor the blow job preceding the calm masked the pain. Rather, new information that I was indeed okay emerged into my awareness. Up until that moment, the state of "okay" had been more than elusive.

And then, shockingly (but in retrospect, not surprisingly) a tidal wave of pain swept through my body. I am not sure where it started or where it went, but it was real, and it hurt—a lot.

I just allowed it to be, felt the pain, and experienced the hurt. Thankfully, when it passed I was still okay, and I still had a quiet mind.

My mind remained quiet for the rest of the day. I decided that I'd had by far my most successful meditation (even though meditation doesn't work in terms of "success" or "failure").

In my meditation practice, I focus my mind on a specific thing—be it energy, breath, sensation, or a blow job—in order to allow some quiet in my mind. When I was receiving that blow job from Ken, I was superbly focused on the sensation on and around my cock and balls. I was concentrating on that one thing, and that concentration was partly what quieted the chatter in my mind.

When I came in Ken's throat, I felt him also being fully conscious, intentionally present, and engaged. Our combined meditative focus created an exchange of energy that was both incredibly pleasurable and quite potent. It opened energetic pathways for both of us and our erotic life force energy—kundalini surged up through my subtle energetic body (the chakra system) and opened me.

Sex is a powerful experience. It's easy and often fun to get lost in the pleasurable sensations. Practicing Tantra with conscious awareness allows me to experience pleasure but not get lost in it. I watch the energy surge through my body from my cock through my belly, my heart, my throat, my third eye, and out my crown chakra, and then back down again through each chakra. Pleasure was the goal, not the distraction from the pain; a tool to focus and deepen my experience of myself. At that moment, I was in a state of grief and pain. I simultaneously felt intense pleasure and pain as it moved throughout my body. The movement of pleasure mixing with and touching pain is healing.

If someone had looked through the window and watched me getting this lovely blow job, he or she wouldn't have seen the energetic exchange. From the outside, it looked like a standard blow job. But from the inside, I could feel a difference. I felt the pleasure we were generating, while my unbearable grief palpably present. My cock was in his mouth while my body hurt. I was sexually and energetically connected to Ken while missing the man who was as essential to my being as my right arm. It wasn't about getting off; it was about ramping up the intensity of pleasure to see if the pleasure principle applied to healing from death and grief.

At first, the pleasure was delightful for my cock, but then I moved that intense pleasure from my hard cock in his mouth to different parts of my body. As if being shot, the pain in my heart and belly suddenly intensified. The blow job wasn't causing pain; it was allowing pain to move. That I was able to bring that specific pleasure to the pain allowing some of the pain to release was very Tantric. The pain couldn't be avoided, suppressed, or masked. I had to face it and feel it. It was the promise I'd made to myself when Zachary died, that I would show up for whatever arose, including the pain.

As we both (from our respective positions of top and bottom) engaged fully in this blow job as meditation, I lost a sense of where I ended and where Ken began. Zachary and I had approached this type of experience with each other, but I think because my heart had been cracked open by his death I was more open with Ken. I needed connection like this to keep me tethered to my body and life. We established a profound energetic link between us. Staying simultaneously present to both sorrow and pleasure was precisely my intention in this experiment.

Ken admitted that he had no idea what this experiment would tell us about how pleasure could affect deep grief. "But," he added, "whenever I am flummoxed, I go back to the principles. When I do this I often find a way out and," he smiled his full-of-faith smile, "I learn new things."

*Sometimes learning new things is exhausting.*

All we could do was stay conscious and collect data from our co-created experiment. One data-point I collected was my superbly quiet mind, which I've never had quite like that before or since. That was immediate data. Later in the day, I realized I was feeling more spacious and energetic in the present moment without being mired in pain. I had a glimpse that there was more to my life than just pain. Bringing pleasure to the pain earlier in the day left me feeling more capable of being present with Zoe and in my life. I was so grateful for this lifeline, and I wholeheartedly wanted to continue the experiment.

About a year after this blow job, one of my clients, who also happens to be a therapist, asked me how I'm able to hold all of the suffering and pain that clients bring into therapy. The question was strangely tricky to answer. While I hold clients' "stuff" with and sometimes for them, I don't feel burdened or weighted down. I wasn't sure how I was doing it. A week and several meditations later, I realized that all I really do is help clients ground their energy. When I sit with a client and listen, I breathe deeply and deliberately down my chakra system through my root chakra bringing the energy down. I metabolize their pain, fear, doubts, concerns, and other agitation, literally releasing it out of my body by grounding. This subtle, quiet, solo energetic process affects their experience both in the room and when they leave my office to live their lives.

When I was able to find words to answer my client's question I recalled that first blow job in the Wailing Room. Ken took the toxic energy—my toxic energy—imbedded in my cum and brought it down to ground. By doing that, he calmed me as well.

The effect is palpable. *As within, so without.* How I move energy inside changes the energy outside of me. Moving my energy changes others' experience as well.

After that morning in the Wailing Room, I had questions and thoughts about what had happened. How did my mind quiet to a level that was so expansive yet comforting? Over chai, Ken and I started to unpack this mystery.

"Remember when you first started studying, you had no idea why we would want to marry yin and yang energies?" Ken asked.

Sheepishly, I remembered that it was not only Zachary who was skeptical. This marriage of yin and yang felt like a slightly more palatable version of the marriage of male and female that was seemingly so central to Tantric practice.

"We did that," Ken reminded me. "I was embodying yin, or receptive energies, and you were embodying yang, or penetrating energies, (once your brain settled and your cock got hard)."

*Right, when I get sucked, there is not much yin about me. I tend to take charge.*

"We each brought these energies to one another. During that exchange, I took charge of pleasuring your cock while you opened up to my wants and desires, and serviced me by feeding me your cock and cum."

I recalled my first hint of the power of energy exchange many years earlier. I was surprised to see how animated a client of mine was when he described how his partner "serviced him." My client was a submissive bottom. My ignorance shone through: I thought that only the top got "serviced" by the bottom. *Energy exchange. Got it.* A lightbulb went off for me as I told Ken about this client.

"So of course, we exchanged energies and our top-ness and bottom-ness became less defining of our experience," I said still trying to unpack the experience.

"Well," he said, "both less defining and more defining. When the exchange is conscious and real, top and bottom, yang and yin, start to transform into one another. The more you became in charge, the more I stepped into my power. The servicer got serviced. Yin and yang, when consciously ramped up, transform.

"What parts go where is less relevant when we play with energies, and playing with energies is Tantra," Ken explained.

The quiet mind; the result of the marriage of yin and yang. This union of yin and yang opens us up to something greater than ourselves. *Sacred. The Divine. God. I got it.* Or at least started to get it, the power of it. I stated what I had heard many, many times and was now glaringly obvious: "Opening to something bigger is why we marry yin and yang."

Ken glanced at me with a slight eye roll and laughed. He knows I am smart but often marveled at how slow I can be. In this case, when we opened up, we each received a quiet, peaceful mind. A sense of being okay, side-by-side with my deep sadness about losing Zachary.

*I came deep in his throat.*

Cum is a potent life force. Cum encompasses all that I am. *As within, so without.*

Using alchemical principles and practices, Ken's ability to ground energy, combined with his psychological savvy, allowed him to transform and ground the highly charged energy of my cum. Our deep and erotic connection, coupled with our energy exchange, transformed and grounded my cum, which calmed and quieted me in ways that decades of meditation had not. After a bit, it calmed Ken as well.

Rituals are deliberate and sacred ceremonies. In a Tantric ritual, we create a container in which we decide what we're going to do for the ritual. We bring the most awareness we can to our intentions for the ritual. The intention might be something we want to create, invite, or change. Then we call in energies that are bigger than we—the gods, the Divine, whatever the words we feel comfortable using.

In Tantra, we often engage erotically to call the gods, drawing them down through our erotic play. Once we call in the gods, we let go and see what happens. When the ritual is over, we thank the energies and "open" the container. Each ritual has a defined beginning, a middle, and a clear and deliberate end. Sometimes the effects of the ritual aren't obvious for days or even weeks or more.

When engaging in ritual, a good rule of thumb is to engage with full awareness of its beginning, middle, and end, and with a clear intention in mind and heart. But sometimes dumb luck or the gods lead you exactly where you need to go. Often what appears to be dumb luck is the gods leading you to exactly where you need to be.

Ken and I had stumbled into creating a ritual space in the Wailing Room. Once we'd experienced the mind-quieting blow job, we each acknowledged the power of our erotic engagement and again decided we would continue this exploration to see what else we could learn. Could regular erotic engagement facilitate my healing? How would Ken be affected? Our boundary had changed. These were not like the erotic healing sessions I'd had with him before.

We talked about our new relationship and decided that I would not pay him for our time in the Wailing Room. Ken was living these principles both personally and professionally. While, like me, he was an expert on grief and loss from a psychotherapeutic perspective, he had never used the principles of Tantra in this way.

He wanted to be there for me as a friend, a teacher, and something more—a partner in healing and a fellow explorer in Tantra. As a teacher and follower of Tantra, helping me through my grief utilizing Tantra was a professional and personal opportunity he had not been previously offered. He had a hunch that we would both learn through our experiments. He offered his knowledge and experience, and I offered an open, yet broken heart, with a willingness to explore. He was curious to see if these tried and true principles could help a dear friend and student heal from the death of his beloved.

Our ritual was established. Ken would arrive early in the morning around 4:30 or 5 AM. We drank chai prepared the same way each morning: with cream and stevia. We took our cups downstairs to the Wailing Room, drank our tea, and talked. We did a brief sitting meditation. The tea preparation, consumption, meditation, and our connecting conversations began our daily ritual. *Beginning*. We set the container for our experiment. Our intention was clear and simple: healing from death. Remaining alive in the face of death. Then we engaged erotically after our meditation. *Middle*. This is where we let go of all expectation, thought, and plans. We surrendered to the mystery of ritual space. Our play invited the gods/goddesses in and we submitted to their/our wisdom.

Finally, we concluded the ritual with my giving Ken some pee. *End*. The act of sharing my pee clearly demarcated the end of what we were doing at that moment.

We sometimes went about our individual days after this; other times he stayed with me as I got Zoe up and off to school. We stayed connected during the day. Either way, the ritual was complete.

Engaging in our ritual, we consciously followed our desire. Ken wanted to be there each morning to minister to me in my suffering. He wanted to be there for himself because he had some inkling that this would help heal him, too. We drank high-quality tea. We enjoyed our conversations. We meditated. We engaged erotically in ways that we both loved and wanted. Our sexual play was never the same day-to-day. We both enjoyed the exchange of energy that came from offering and receiving pee. By following of our desires—a core principle of Tantrists—we set up a healing ritual that saved my life.

*Beginning, middle, and end.*

# CHAPTER 12

*He died that day because his body had served its purpose.*
*His soul had done what it came to do, learned what it*
*came to learn, and then was free to leave.*

—*Garth Stein*
*The Art of Racing in the Rain*

A COUPLE OF months after Zachary's death, his brother hosted a memorial at his home on the beach up north. It was a beautiful day with a bonfire burning on the tide flats that was extinguished by the incoming tide to symbolize Zachary's death.

People spoke, food was shared, and tears were shed. What I remember most about the day was talking with an acquaintance who was about my age, and who had lost his partner about six months earlier to a prolonged battle with cancer. He asked if I had had any dreams about Zachary yet.

I had not. Even in my dreams, he was decidedly absent. Friends and family had experienced dreams with Zachary. He was snowboarding, cooking, teaching, laughing, and drinking wine. I had not seen him. I wanted to see him, even if only in my dreams.

The hours of each day dragged. Time moved slowly. Yet at the same time, it felt like Zachary had been dead for years... or forever.

A journal entry:

> *I am at day 10. It feels like years. Something like dog years: death years. One day feels like a couple of years. I have been in this semi-alive, fully painful, mostly over-whelmed, scared, sad, sad place. The sadness is so deep that I do not know where it lives. But it is inside of me, and it has smashed my core. My sense of me seems elusive.*
>
> *Who am I? If not part of the Me, Zachary, Zoe family, then who am I? All of the big life things I do (real estate, father, Tantra, architecture, design, therapist, landlord, manager, etc.) I do in the context of my place in this family: Me, Zachary, Zoe. Now, with no Zachary, who am I?*
>
> *How does my life work?*

In Tantric terms, my third chakra (the chakra of who I am in the world) had been compromised, broken (although I know chakras cannot break). In other words, my stomach ached, hurt, a lot of the time. Zoe's did too. Many times each day she would tell that me her stomach hurt. All I could do was hold her and tell her, "I know honey... So does mine."

I hated feeling powerless to help her make her experience different, better. Every time I leaned into my belly, the tears flowed. My body convulsed with the pain. I shook and cried.

*Who am I without Zachary? I have no idea. That is now my "work." How do I take a journey back to myself when I have no idea where to start or where I am going? Oh, right, my heart is broken beyond words. The pain seems to start in my guts and screeches to a halt in my heart.*

I began to notice a strange phenomenon that accompanied my tremendous loss. Time had stopped, and paradoxically, it didn't. If it had, I might have felt some relief from its relentless momentum. Perhaps the importance I gave time had been temporarily suspended. Or perhaps I had lost the anchors that allowed me to track the movement of the sun, the earth, the pages of the calendar, and the hands on a clock. Hours and days both flew by and took on an excruciating eternity.

Someone wrote a card to me:

> *It's not that seconds don't tick and minutes don't creep— they still do, but only relevant to a world that in the context of loss ceases to be relevant.*

Most of what happened around me ceased to be relevant. I had no familiar anchor to judge time. No fixed point from which to perceive the motion of life. What had once seemed important relative to time ceased to be.

Everything except my moment-to-moment existence stopped. Projects put on hold. Mail not retrieved. Bills noticed, but not paid. Deadlines missed. Calls unanswered. Clients notified I was down for the count. Daily life stopped. And yet, strangely and thankfully, the seconds, minutes, and days continued to tick.

In effect, time, which had been formerly oriented toward and enforced by external factors, flipped back to being internally oriented or more precisely, just disoriented. I simply could not care about anything beyond the absurdity, complexity, raw simplicity, and surreality of my present experience, my pain, and Zoe.

"Life goes on." This was one of those irritating cliché truths about death—even traumatic sudden death. Friends said (thoughtfully and thoughtlessly) but always with good intention, "Life goes on," as though that sentiment somehow is comforting. It never was.

People (friends, family, and strangers alike) living their post-Zachary lives was jarring. *Life does go on, but how? I have no idea. Why? I sort of know why, but not really.* Nothing looked or felt the same to me. I was always (although not always pleasantly) surprised by day-to-day life. The grocery store, driving, school drop-off and pick-up, walking along the beach, were all experiences filled with people living their lives. The mundane day-to-day activities of others' lives bothered me. The mundane day-to-day activities of my life became both meaningless and profoundly meaningful all at once. *Life goes on.*

I was shocked that people could go on when I was carrying all of this pain. My pain felt like a loud, blinding, neon beacon. It was not. It was a very quiet, personal, intimate, and solo experience. I am not sure if that was comforting or angering or both. Even though I was deeply connected to Ken as I groped around for my new life, it was a profoundly solo and lonely experience. *Zachary is dead, and people are actually continuing to live as though nothing in their lives have changed? How could this be? Mindfuck. Life goes on.*

Mostly everyone other than Zoe, me, and Ken had returned to their mostly normal lives. This is not to say that people were not affected or devastated or deeply moved—many were. People moving back to their lives was precisely what we all needed. But it again reminded me that life goes on. *God, I hate those three words strung together. Life. Goes. On.* My life as I knew it, had stopped dead.

Zachary's brothers and sisters were clearly devastated by the loss of their brother, but their lives appeared, at least on the outside, to be back to normal. They were working and putting on good faces for the people in their lives. Because of everyone's financial generosity, I had the luxury of time when they did not.

Their lives were calling them, demanding them, to be back in the game and functioning properly. For those lucky to have any bereavement benefits at work, three days of leave is not uncommon when a loved one passes.

Zoe and I saw his family often, and those times were uncomfortably comfortable. Zachary was our connection to these families, and he was noticeably gone. They were my family, yet the adults among us knew how tenuous our connection was in the absence of Zachary.

As a parent, I was for the first time glad that Zachary's parents had died long before I joined the family. I would not have wanted them to experience the most horrible of all losses—the loss of their son.

I was experiencing my own death, too. I was no longer a therapist. I was no longer designing and managing the construction of our home; I was no longer a bicycle rider; I was no longer doing real estate deals; I was no longer an architecture snob; I no longer tracked the financial world. I was a stay-at-home dad and not a very interesting one at that. I could no longer be the man I was without being defined by the man I lost. I was no longer a husband; I was no longer a co-parent; I was no longer Zachary's lover and bed partner. What was lost is still a significant thread in the tapestry that is me. Given Zoe's age when Zachary died, I often wonder to what extent her loss of him will define who she becomes.

In the last year of her life, my aunt Rose said she was "bored and boring." Her body was slowly failing, and her strength was waning. Her life grew smaller each day, and she engaged less and less. She was bored of the monotony of her life, and when she related to the world, she was boring because she could only speak of the nuanced day-to-day progression of her body's demise. I experienced this "bored and boring" life after Zachary died. My life was boring in that I was only focused on my pain and my experience of my pain. It was relentless.

During the 2008 Democratic primary season, Zachary had been a die-hard Obama supporter. He thought Obama could and should win the nomination. I was a Clinton fan. We had many spirited arguments among ourselves and with friends.

After Zachary died, Hillary Clinton motioned to nominate Barack Obama to be the Democratic candidate for President of the Unites States. Bear Sterns collapsed, Obama was leading a spirited campaign, and some of our most powerful leaders thought Sarah Palin could run the country. I was only peripherally aware of these momentous happenings. I was aware of my body, my pain, my pleasure, Zoe's needs, and her experience of first grade. I had become my aunt Rose: I was bored with the same story each day and boring with the retelling of the same story each day—always pain, sorrow, fear, and grief.

At the same time, I was deep into an exploration of Tantra. I did not yet know how to be in the world that was outside the Wailing Room. While my exploration was deeply rich and satisfying (and not boring at all), it was an exploration for which I had no words that would make sense to many of my family and friends. I still don't. Although deeply connected to Ken, I was on a solo journey.

As I deepened my practice of Tantra, using the erotic to heal, I grew more apart from much of the world around me. I was not able to share my path with my community. I did not know how to speak about my dogged determination in engaging erotic pleasures, as my body, mind, and soul reorganized everything in my world. *All in response to death and grief.*

When I thought too much about it, Tantra made little sense to me. But when I felt it and gathered data from what I was doing, it made all the sense in the world.

My Tantric practice was my lifeline and paradoxically caused even more loss. Each of my relationships changed after Zachary's death and during my healing. Close friends of Zachary and mine could not (or would not) understand my deep erotic and heart connection to Ken. It looked to many like I was dishonoring Zachary and his memory by being in a new relationship... *A new relationship? As if I could be in a partner-type relationship immediately following Zachary's death? Really?*

Some close friends drifted. Other close friends were supportive, but they were living their day-to-day lives, and their lives did not include a frequent conscious embrace of the erotic—they had nothing in their lives that opened any doors to understanding my experiences. They were at a loss as to how to connect with me in any real way. I had few words to describe my experience to those not on this path.

*More loss. The losses are compounding.*

The unexpected collateral loss of friends and confidantes and my day-to-day connection with them, paradoxically hardly registered. Although those losses paled in comparison to the loss of Zachary, they still hurt like hell. Losing my husband and Zoe losing her dad were separate from the foibles of ego, drama, and judgment. My loss of Zachary was deep, a soul-level loss. On the other hand, smaller, less primary losses also hurt, but very differently. *Can I count on nothing? Can I depend on no one to hold steady? Are no structures in my life solid? Apparently not.* I needed steady, and some of my closest people could not hold steady as I moved through my days.

*Compounding losses.*

I am not sure if friends drifted because of my Tantra work with Ken, or if they drifted because many people do not know how to relate to people who are deeply grieving. Death is frightening to many of us. Some friends who drifted had no idea about my relationship with Ken, while others knew the details quite intimately.

Ken and I would show up together at Zoe's school, at social gatherings, at our home when I was packing to move, at the local food truck for lunch, or when out to dinner. Ken knew me intimately and was willing to hold my hand as I stumbled around trying to find my new life. He held me steady.

To most, we looked like best friends. We were. To my most intimate friends, we looked like lovers. We were. Gay friends had an intuitive sense of how we could be intimate lovers and not partners, while straight friends had no frame of reference for intense sexual intimacy coupled with friendship outside the container of "relationship." While it was not always easy, we each knew the container of our relationship was about healing, learning, and exploration.

Part of my problem with building community was that I did not know how to connect with people outside of Zoe and Ken. *Who am I if I am not Zachary's husband?* I learned that I had no wisdom about how to be an intimate friend without him. I was clumsy. I was certainly messy. I was indeed focused on myself and my pain. I was bored and boring.

*And Tantra. I was focused on Tantra.*

In the universal balancing act, friends who were less intimate showed up in ways that astounded. Some genuinely wanted to know more about what I was doing to heal. They were not afraid of me, my pain, my path, or my sex. They saw the wreckage of my life. They were able to stay present with me even in the rubble. They were amazed by "the clarity... the intensity" in my eyes. Many newer people in my life noted respect for how I was carrying out my day-to-day life when in their minds, they could not do it with the grace with which I was living.

I was carrying out my life by practicing Tantra each day for a couple of hours, sometimes more, and moving a lot of energy. I processed a lot each day. Tantra is about all kinds of pleasure, not just sexual pleasure.

Ken and I shared other pleasures like walking on the beach and eating out. We embraced the healing power of pleasure. We consciously brought pleasure to where I hurt. People were afraid of me and my pain. When I cried around some people, they thought they had upset me. When I was in pain and people could not comfort me (little was, in fact, comforting), they felt uncomfortable; and then I felt uncomfortable. My life became more out of sync with the rest of the world. Death is more than a bit isolating.

In some ways, my life is still is out of sync. Not only did he die, but the problem is that he remains dead.

When people who knew and loved Zachary saw me, they expected me to be in the same shape I was when they last saw me. They were conflicted: they could see that I was healing with each visit, and they saw me in an intimate relationship with Ken. Some felt loyalty to their memory of Zachary. It was confusing to those who didn't see me regularly or at least hang out occasionally with Ken and me. The combination of profound grief and intense Tantric practice left me somewhat disconnected from my community. Ken often reminded me that, "Tantra is not an easy path." *Indeed, it is not.*

The new people in my life called every day, often ate meals with us, invited us to join their circle of loved ones, got drunk with me, laughed with me, listened to stories of then and now, and made space for me to heal in ways I thought best. They were lifelines.

Years later, the chasm exists. I know what I know about life and death because I experienced this loss. I would not wish it on anyone. Yet, as the years tick by, more of us join Life After Death Club. Being a club member makes me both more accessible and more separate.

Death is isolating. Being unabashedly sexual in the modern world is isolating. Combining sex and death is profoundly isolating. It took me the better part of a year to engage in the world in what seemed like (to an observer) a normal, healthy manner. I needed almost three years to feel any semblance of "normal" in my new normal life.

I am in the world in the way I am now because I experienced traumatic loss. New people who enter my life and did not know Zachary, or my life with him, cannot know me deeply. The chasm is alive and well.

I live where I live, I parent the way I parent, I eat the way I eat, I love the way I love, I fuck the way I fuck, I look the way I look, I work the way I work all because I lived through the loss of the man I loved most. I love my life now. I loved my life then. And that is a little fucked up because my life would not be what it is today if Zachary were alive.

*Mindfuck.*

Tantra engaged my primal, creative, and powerful life force—even when I was not sure how, or why, or what to do. Tantra nurtured my resilience. It was not an easy engage-ment. It often hurt like hell and hastened many more losses, but Tantra opened me for a new life I had not previously known or imagined.

# CHAPTER 13

*A good orgasm is satisfying, but a great orgasm can be
a revelation of your deepest being, unfolding the truth
of who you are...*

—David Deida

ZACHARY AND I had purchased a stunningly beautiful
twenty-four-acres of pristine, forested, waterfront land on a
neighboring island in Puget Sound. The land on which we
were planning to build our home had rolling hills, streams,
beachfront, and an old-growth tree. The land was magical.
During the two years preceding his death, Zachary and I got
to know every nook and cranny of the acreage. We talked
endlessly about our planned home, parties we would have,
afternoons on the beach—a good life. I had only been to the
property a couple of times without him. Our goal had been
to move in before his fortieth birthday party. He particularly
liked this idea.

After two long years of working with architects and county
regulatory agencies, we had our permit to break ground and
begin construction of our road and utility placement. Our
loan was a day or two from being funded. We had arrived.

Then he was killed. The project was not killed but put on hold—indefinitely. *Kind of killed. More loss.*

The land was healing, chock full of plans, dreams, and (I now knew) assumptions. We assumed that we would be alive. We assumed that we would live there. We assumed that Zachary would take care of the trail that meandered from the home site down to the beach. We assumed that I would get the house built. We assumed that we would spend our week-ends hiking down to the beach, playing, talking, and exploring. We assumed we would gather friends and family for food and wine... We assumed that he (and I for that matter) would not die for a few, or maybe many, decades.

About a month after his death, I had no palpable desire to go to our land yet felt strangely compelled to visit. I went. The day was filled with polarities and paradoxes.

The spot was stunningly beautiful. *How can it not be?* Yet, it was ugly. *How can it not be?* It was healing and heart-breaking, strange and foreign, yet it felt like home. A storm must have come through since my last visit; things were different. Zachary had done some thorough trail maintenance the week before he died. *Did he die? Yes. He died. Shit, he did. But the trail looks so well maintained? Is it true? Is it possible? What the fuck?*

I could not imagine not living there, and yet living there seemed utterly unimaginable without Zachary. The place was so overwhelmingly lonely, beautiful, dark, light, alive, and dead.

There was the paradox—alive and dead all at once, a snap-shot of my life, of my insides.

I spoke out loud to him. *With him?* I cried and cried while I was speaking. Shortly after arriving at the land, I realized that I went with the hope or expectation that I would see or feel him in a meaningful way. I did not. I did, however, profoundly experience the lack of him. *Oh, that again.* I was speaking out loud to a dead man whom I could not feel in any way.

*Mindfuck. He remains dead.*

My life at that moment was all about him (or more accurately—the lack of him). Zachary no longer existed. Yet it was his not existing that was the focus of my every waking moment. I was very much engaged with him even though he was not there.

He was very alive in me, yet clearly, he was not. He did not exist. *Fuck. That is a hard concept.*

The fact that pleasure, sexual pleasure, was my tether to being alive and grounded also struck me as paradoxical. Engaging the erotic as sacred seemed paradoxical. Fucking so I could feel pain more acutely seemed paradoxical. The only thing that made any sense was that feeling pain deeply was the path to releasing and healing from it. Trying to avoid pain is most often what lands clients in my office with a life that no longer works for them. I did not want my life to become organized by my desire to avoid pain. I knew that avoidance is a dead end.

---

I WANTED TO bring the land (this huge part of our lives) somehow into my healing work. The land kept feeling far away, yet part of my soul and essence. So a few weeks later, I brought Ken to the land with the intention of practicing Tantra. I was curious to see what would emerge as Ken and I were there together.

I wanted to see, or feel really, the gardens at our previous home before we headed to the new land. Zachary and I had lived there together for twelve years, tending the gardens just out of sight of the water. It was the only true home I knew with Zachary. Ken and I started our day in the gardens of our old home.

Being there with Ken started to alter my consciousness. I felt Zachary's presence which was both comforting and painful. I "saw" him— well, I did not literally. In my mind's eye (or was it real?) I kept seeing his generously proportioned hands at the base of plants. In my mind's ear, I heard him say, as he had said hundreds of times, "You know, I should really be a hand model."

My third eye was vibrating. I so wanted to see him, yet not seeing him, the alive him, made my stomach hurt. He loved his hands touching the earth. I saw his hands—no question.

My heart was heavy. It was wonderful to see the gardens after our two-year absence, but these gardens were no longer ours. We had left them to the new owners, who had been keeping them up well. This visit to the old place helped facilitate another letting go of my life with Zachary.

Then Ken and I headed off to our land. *Wait—my land, not our land...Oh god, can I do this?* That language was so hard to own. *My Zoe. My land. My life. My bed. My house. My future.* It did not flow. I choked on it, stumbling around this small shift in language.

Revisiting the land with with Ken was both wonderful and awful with all of the plans for a future that no longer existed. *The house will sit here, cars go here, see the view from here, we are trying to save this tree here. We are going to grow food here.* I had to own all of the pain of what was not here and invite Ken to hold it with me so that I could begin to let go. Let go of the dreams. Let go of the vision of the land and our lives as stewards of this land. Let go of "our." Let go of the house plans. Let go of Zachary and our life together.

*The problem is he remains dead.*

We stopped at the top of a knoll, in the shadow of a 300-year-old Douglas Fir tree, about 175 feet back from the Sound on a tiny, flat spot filled with tall, oddly-straight trees. We felt physically small.

Ken and I had been talking all morning on the way to the old house, and then at what was now my land. We became quiet. A wave of bittersweet nostalgia swept over me.

Ken dropped to his knees. I gave him my cock. As he began to suck me, all of the feelings, the old garden, the new land, the plans, my loss, my fears, started swirling around in my body. I felt overwhelmed, lost, on shaky ground. I was delighting in the sexual play, yet I was seemingly all messed up inside—adrift and scared. I was in a swirl of past and present and worry about future. Disoriented, I started to panic. Then I remembered my practice. I did what I knew to do. I breathed and continued to give Ken my cock—and breathed some more.

I thought I might pass out from the swirling in my head and guts. As I came, I looked up at the sky. I saw indescribable beauty—trees, light, and color. I smelled the peaty ground, the salty water, the decay, and the sap. I heard the waves and the birds. My energy first shot out through my crown chakra toward the sky; a few moments later it went down into the damp fertile ground through my root chakra. I was connected or part of all of the perfection (or God) around me. I *was* the perfection that was around me. I was not separate from the beautiful, complex living/dying cycle of Earth, and of the magnificent, awe-inspiring Consciousness of the Sky—*as within so without*. I felt it—at one with all that was around me. *Unitary Consciousness. God.* I was not separate from Ken, the trees, the sky, the dirt, loss, my cum, the water. I was all of that and more.

Intellectually I knew that this sort of connection with *all that is* is possible. I believed it might be possible actually to embody this connection, maybe for other people, not me—but still possible. I had been meditating for over twenty years with the hope of some sort of transcendental experience. I am not a very good meditator. I am not good at being of quiet mind. I am not good at seeing, feeling, or experiencing God around me. But apparently, when one needs to feel a connection with *all that is*, one simply does.

I had another experience of profound quiet.

And of deep pain—this time the pain felt like I was on morphine—aware of the pain with pinpoint accuracy, but, while not pleasant it did not bother or alarm me. My pain was a part of a bigger picture; one that I could only begin to understand.

All was okay. All was beautiful. How could I not know the world was okay when my energy was flowing with uninhibited ease in my body, and the earth around me was absolutely stunning?

I was also aware that even in the most alive and pristine natural setting, death and decay are woven into the landscape. *As within, so without.* So it was with me. I was alive, at peace, and woven through this peaceful aliveness, the pleasures of the body, and calm, was my not-subtle awareness of death: Zachary's death, and the death of so much in my life.

I was physically and energetically open. The gross sexual play followed by the more subtle energetic openings had me exquisitely present in that moment. There were no blocks or separations between me, Ken (my soft cock still held in his mouth), the earth, and the sky. The flow between them was easy, and felt good. It allowed access to my pain in a way that facilitated letting go. *Trust.*

This time was the second since Zachary's death that I trusted all was okay. Not only was I going to be okay at some point in the coming years, but I was okay in the present. Death and life were woven into me—optimism and life dancing with despair and fear.

Our erotic service of one another once again physically and energetically opened me to something greater than my own experience. It opened us to the world of the gods. His throat chakra servicing my second chakra, and my cock servicing his throat. The link between these two chakras was connected and firing, setting us up for a marriage of energies; the inner marriage of yin and yang.

Add my now sacred, emotion-filled cum to the mix and a very powerful inner/outer marriage happened. When Ken took my cum, his energy grounded through his root chakra as my energy went up, and my crown chakra opened. As that pathway was established between Ken and me (an energetic "marriage"), I was able to ground through my root chakra while he was able to open to consciousness through his crown chakra. We used our "outer marriage" (cock in mouth) to assist our inner marriages of yin and yang so that we each experienced our sacred sexual energy move both up and down our chakra systems. The most powerful and pleasurable part of our sexual play together was after we slowed; in this case, after I came. My cumming was pleasurable, but that pleasure was dwarfed by the movement of the mutually generated erotic energy up and down my body.

Tantric sex has always been about energetic and physically opening. In what at first seems like a paradox, penetrative sex always physically, emotionally, and energetically opens me regardless of whether I am penetrating or being penetrated.

The penetrator becomes the penetrated; yin and yang energies are not static and as they move, they morph into one another. Through penetrating, I allow myself to be energetically penetrated; that subtle penetration literally and physically opens me. As I open, the delicious sexual energy we generate flows easily.

In my mind's eye, it looks like a chimney sweep is going up and down the central channel near my spine. Energetic blocks (of which there are often many) are swept away. Erotic play is the chimney sweep that opens my body and clears the pathway for the movement of subtle energies.

Once I am open physically through penetrating or being penetrated, the gross eroticism, while super fun, is less necessary. Once energetically open, the subtle energies, connections, and marriages come into play—which is what opens us energetically to the gods. Or, one could also say, as Ken often did, "The gross play sets the stage for the gods and the subtle energies are the gods playing and delighting in our eroticism."

I was beginning to understand the whole-body orgasm. Clearly, it was nothing like I imagined.

While the ride to the destination is pretty wild, sexy, and big, Tantra is about what happens once the energies become subtle. Awareness of, and engagement with, subtle energies is a practice that requires focused attention to one's body, a quiet mind, and focused breath.

And it feels akin to bliss. *Connection. Pleasure. God.*

# CHAPTER 14

*Death ends a life, not a relationship.*

—*Mitch Albom*
*Tuesdays with Morrie*

AS HALLOWEEN APPROACHED, I indulged my long-time curiosity by asking Ken if he would be willing to engage in a conscious erotic ritual with me. I was not surprised to hear Ken say, "Sure! Tell me more." I didn't know much more than I wanted to learn about erotic ritual. Given the season, we talked about how the veil between the dead and the living supposedly becomes more porous, thinner, around Halloween. I was still missing Zachary and was not surprisingly frustrated about my experience of only feeling his absence, as opposed to others who feel the presence of their departed loved ones. His "presence" was elusive to me; I was yearning to see, feel, or experience something of Zachary's essence. Ken was curious.

Of course I was aware that Zachary was dead so that seeing him or feeling him was a ridiculous hope. By this point in my grieving process I knew that dead meant dead; he no longer existed. But I couldn't help this nagging feeling I had that I was missing... something.

Could erotic ritual somehow help me?

We decided to engage in this ritual on Halloween. *Just go for what you want, right? Follow your desire, right? I am fucking nuts, right?*

Early that the evening, Ken and I met with two other Tantric practitioners for a visit and meditation. For about an hour we meditated together; then in the spirit of play we each imbibed some spirits (mostly Hendricks gin and whiskey).

After some laughter, conversation, and sips, the group decided that I was to be anointed with the spirits in preparation for our impending ritual. I entered into the center of the impromptu circle, and each of my fellow explorers anointed me with a bit of spirits and well-wishes to send me off into the night. I was anointed on my head, my heart, my belly, and my crotch. They held Ken and me as we left the circle and headed on to our evening of ritual.

This gathering embodied what I was growing to know about Tantra—playful (spirits and all), loving, supporting, and decidedly not rule-bound or fundamentalist. We accessed the power of group meditation; we talked about our lives through the lens of the principles and practices of our lineage of Tantra. What stuck out to me the most at that part of the evening was how interested and available I was to hear about others' lives—this was a part of me I had not experienced since Zachary's death. The circle reminds me that something a little larger than my own experience with pleasure and healing is at work; it reminds me of community and how vital community is to our well-being.

Because neither Ken nor I considered ourselves to be skilled at ritual, we asked these folks for help. One helped focus our

attention by asking what we wanted to let into our lives and/
or release from our lives. He believes that embodying one's
intentions is not only the cornerstone of most ritual but also
of one's growth and development as a conscious person.

Together, the four of us continued this exploration of intention and ritual, as well as generating ideas for how to embody
our intentions.

I was clear (or perhaps my skeptic side was clear). I wanted
to bring in Zachary. I was feeling alone and lost in my new
world. I knew he was gone—I had not a shred of denial. I
was repeatedly and brutally experiencing his absence, and I
wanted to experience his presence. I had experienced both
the finality of his death (the "game over feeling"), as well as
the palpable presence of his absence. The game was over. Yet
"leaks" of our knowing about his impending death left me
unsure. There had to be more than 'game over'. 'Game over'
did not adequately explain my experiences both before and
after his death.

While studying Tantra, I held my skeptical nature right
alongside my curiosity. *Are we the gods? Do the gods want
us to play? Is this really just one of many planes of existence?
After we die, is game not over?*

For my emerging life to be fulfilling and interesting, I needed
to let go of the concept of family that had held me (held us) so
well. I needed to let go of the family as me, Zachary, and Zoe
as this particular family structure no longer existed. I knew
any real freedom in my new life would elude me if I failed at
the task of letting go, and I needed freedom. "Zachary, Zoe
and Me" was no longer my family, and my body was struggling to catch up with that reality—a pointedly difficult letting

go. Yet letting go of that reality was real and necessary. I desired freedom, so I embraced the path that made the most sense— letting go. *Through letting go? This particular letting go? Really? Fuck. This is a hard path to embrace.*

Before I could let go, I wanted a real connection with Zachary. Those who knew and loved me understood that I am quite concrete in my thinking and body. For years, family and friends called me "concrete head." When I don't experience something in my body, I do not know it exists. I had on my concrete head. I wanted, needed, connection with Zachary to move on. This was my intention entering the ritual.

*Simple. A good intention for my first Tantric ritual... Am I setting myself up for another let down? I need to let go regardless if I connect with a dead man. I am losing my mind.*

Since he died, I had been looking for Zachary everywhere. I looked for him at the store, the farmer's market, our land, his and Zoe's school, in the eyes of his siblings, my bed, on caller ID, in Zoe's eyes, and on, and on, and on. *Relentless.* I was growing weary of looking for him and yet could not, would not—did not want to stop looking. So, I decided I would look for him in ritual space as well.

My goals for our ritual were clear: look for Zachary and let go of all that was home to me. *Good times, eh?*

Ken and I left the group and headed to my shell of a home. After some conversation about our ritual, we embarked. The beginning was marked by the setting of a circle—an energetic (and sometimes physical) space in which ritual is performed. We called in energies from the five elements: fire, water, air/ether, earth, and metal.

I had collected dirt from Zachary's and my favorite potted Japanese maple tree to call in earth energies. We burned incense that Zachary had around the house to call in air/the ethers. We used urine, from both Ken and me, to call water energy. We burned a candle to call fire. I placed Zachary's wedding band on the altar to call the energy of metal. I placed some of pictures of him on the altar. Gathering these items was brutal. The ring, the tree, the photos, were all filled with stories and history. Seeing the things we had gathered on the altar made me feel vulnerable. Despite all I had shared with Ken, I felt oddly strange allowing him to see this altar. It was like Ken could see right through me to my emptiness, my pain, my sorrow. Given the depth of my sharing with Ken, being seen so raw in this moment was disquieting, as if I had been split open for easy viewing. But while uncomfortable, I am sure this transparency was positive.

*Can I fucking leave? Can I run? I want to vomit. Breathe... Just breathe...*

While Ken and I were placing the items on the altar, we asked each energy to be present with us, to hold and help us with transformation. All of these activities (including my desire to run) combine to set the circle, create energetic boundaries, to help contain the energy and intentions of the ritual.

Ken and I had decided that instead of prescribing specific erotic and non-erotic behaviors for our ritual, we would just engage erotically by following our desires. We decided to play erotically for some amount of time and see what, if anything, would happen.

Our circle was set. We undressed and began engaging, awkwardly, self consciously.

Although Ken and I had been having sex to varying degrees each day for months, I felt particularly shy as we brought our naked bodies together on this Halloween evening. Tonight was different as our bodies seemed to not quite know what to do. Hands strayed here and there; movement and stillness danced awkwardly. I took some deep breaths to ground.

I felt the urge to begin slowly scratching Ken's back and sides. I am not sure how or why I did this other than I was following desire; a desire I had never experienced. I started firmly, and he responded by melting with pleasure. I increased my pressure and intensity, and he melted into my fingers some more. I began to get aroused. The harder I dug into his skin the more turned on I got, the more pleasure he experienced. The pleasure was intoxicating.

We set up an energy exchange that was deeply pleasurable to each of us from seemingly opposite energy sources. I was engaging more yang, giving, penetrating energies while Ken was engaging more yin, receptive, receiving energies. Soon into this exchange, he was unambiguously surrendering to me, which was giving me pleasure—I was scratching him, and he was receiving long, hot, red marks along his body. I was administering pain in a deliberate and loving fashion and, in his surrender to this sensation, he was experiencing ecstatic pleasure. Who knew that slow, intense, and deliberate scratching could offer each of us whole-body pleasure like neither of us had experienced?

I was beginning to get the knack of whole-body orgasms, which, as I was discovering, are far more intense and pleasurable than ejaculating, lasting longer and longer with each practice. I was unambiguously experiencing whole-body pleasure from this play. While we each were quite hard, we were not engaging with our cocks at all.

Ken was lying on top of me, and I was scratching his sides. The dark red lines on him were stunningly hot. All of a sudden his face changed; it relaxed, then contorted. His eyes lost focus.

"What just happened?" I asked.

He thought for a moment, "I just felt some pressure on my back, and I don't know much more than that. It caught me by surprise."

I continued scratching. We were both enjoying this new play we had stumbled upon.

Then, in a voice that was not quite Ken's, he said, "Wow, you have never done this before... I am loving this, and it's a bit scary... you are teaaarrring my insides up... this hurts... a lot... "

While I love erotically administering pain I, paradoxically, do not enjoy hurting anyone.

Suddenly Ken was not experiencing the pain as pleasure, so I stopped. Staring quite intensely into my eyes, he said, "Please. Please continue. Please. I need to hurt right now."

He unequivocally wanted more. His discomfort scared and disoriented me. I gave him more of what he wanted—pain. I was hurting him. I increased my intensity, hurting him more. I began to feel confused. The level of pressure and intensity frightened me; yet, I was compelled to do more, and harder. I was now close to drawing blood.

"You are not going to like this, but... I have to go... " He covered my eyes so I couldn't see him and he began weeping. "I have to go... We had a good run... I have to leave... I loved our time together... It meant more than you know... I have to go... I am so sorry... I know this is not what you want... I have to go... I can't stay... "

Disoriented does not begin to describe my swirl of emotions and thoughts. I asked him, almost pleaded with him, to stay. He said no. I was frightened and pulled back from Ken. "Please don't go now. I don't understand. I don't want you to go."

"I know... I know it's not what you want... I have to go... It hurts so much... my insides are torn up ... I'm scared... "

I was crying. He was crying. We both had unusually, almost painfully, hard cocks. I cannot imagine that this was actually true, but in my body's memory, I am sure our cocks were larger than they had been before. *And hard, hard, hard.* In that moment, I did not know why I was crying.

He kept talking about needing to go, but it was clear that Ken was not going anywhere.

"I have to go... "

With me on my back and Ken on top of me I placed my hard cock on his belly—precisely where he said he hurt. *Bring pleasure to the spots that hurt. Bring pleasure to the pain. The healing power of pleasure. I know how to do this.* I knew that bringing pleasure to pain worked. I used my hard cock to press into his belly, to fuck his belly. I was compelled to bring the energy of my cock to the place that was hurting him. At the instant I firmly pressed my cock in to his belly, his eyes rolled back into his head, and he collapsed on top of me. Then, just as quickly, he bolted upright wide-eyed and confused.

Suddenly, we each had soft cocks. As surprising as it had been that we were hard and big, it was even more surprising how quickly we became un-hard. In that moment, I felt as though everything had tilted on its axis.

Sheepishly I said, "I did not want you to go."

Ken looked at me confused. "I'm not going anywhere," he said calmly and clearly. He had no idea why I said this.

The reality hit me like a ton of bricks. I burst into tears. I had been talking to Zachary—not Ken. My tears only further confused Ken.

*I have to go...*

When Zachary was hit by the car, he was thrown ninety-four feet. His legs were broken, his face and head badly bruised, and he had internal bleeding in his belly. The three-hour surgery he endured had only focused on stopping the bleeding *in his belly*. The bleeding in his belly needed to stop, or he would die. Since he was teetering on the edge of life and death, he couldn't be fully anesthetized. The doctors could not get the bleeding to stop. It was this bleeding in his belly that ultimately killed him.

*His belly must have hurt like hell during those last hours.*

The change in Ken's face and demeanor, the pressure he felt on his back, triggered by my scratching along and around his midsection, suddenly made sense. Zachary was saying goodbye. He was feeling his insides being torn, and he was struggling to leave. He was leaving me, leaving Zoe, and leaving all he knew.

Leaving was not easy for him. I like to think some deaths are easy, and I had thought he had only a couple of seconds of consciousness before he died—making his death, while tragic, a little easier. But now I know that he struggled leaving us, and his death was painful. This knowledge breaks my heart; it makes me sick to my stomach.

When I told Ken what had happened, he remembered it as a dream with vague familiarity. Beyond that, he had no recollection of pain, crying, wanting to leave, or our erotic play. He had some sense that our playing involved me scratching him, but he had no memory of it, no lingering sense of having been scratched. His body was shockingly mark-free; as though I had not been scratching him just shy of drawing blood.

*What the fuck? How did the sear marks disappear? I know I saw them. I know what I did to him. I know I was concerned about drawing blood. How is his skin mark free?*

About ten minutes later while we were standing by the bed talking, his face suddenly changed again.

He got in my face in an uncharacteristically aggressive manner and said, "Don't be afraid... don't be afraid." Over and over, "Don't be afraid; don't be afraid." His demeanor was terrifying.

Ken never got in my face about anything. My mind took a few seconds to catch up; this was not Ken in my face. While it was terrifying, I heard him and was able to absorb the message.

*Don't be afraid.*

My predominant experience since Zachary's death had been unmitigated fear. I was afraid that I would not know how to be a single parent, that I would not know how to take care of my Zoe, and that I would not know how to take care of my broken self.

*Afraid. How do I wake her* up? *How do I get her to school? How do I feed her? How do we talk about our loss? How do we talk about our lives? How do I help her with math? How do I not break down every time I see the loss in her eyes? Fear, pure and unadulterated. How do I keep us alive and well in such a scary world where terrible things happen?*

Now Zachary, through Ken, was in my face telling me not to be afraid.

Instantly I was no longer terrified. Ken stepped back and relaxed. He smiled. I smiled. I had some awareness that what

I was seeing and feeling was crazy, and began to allow my skeptical mind to catch up.

Then Zachary, through Ken said, "I'm glad we got that time together." I teared up. He was talking about our recent trip to Europe. "It's okay. You always worry, and you don't need to… We had a good run."

He referred to Zoe by the nickname that only he called her; I was startled hearing that name from Ken's mouth. "You gave me the best of life: Zoe, you, adventure, travel, and family. When we met Zoe's mom for the first time, I knew it was all going to be fine when you were just nuts with worry. Thank you."

I hoarsely responded, "Thank you." It felt so shallow to have no more words.

"You are my best friend," he said.

I wept. "I love you, and have no doubt how much you love me."

That clarity of his love for me and my love for him was a life preserver both in that moment and for years to follow. It was heart-wrenching and crystal clear.

Just as I began to experience a vague sense of fear about what was happening with Ken, he returned, and Zachary was once again gone. Ken's face and voice returned to normal, and once again, he had no memory of what had transpired—only a vague dream-like sense of events that he could only recall in response to my recounting them.

Without ending the ritual, we decided to take a break by going to the kitchen for a drink. Seeing Ken change so profoundly frightened me. Ken looked peaked; it was evident that this process was taxing his body. I suggested we end the ritual.

I could have stopped. In fact, the experience was just disquieting enough that I was becoming afraid again but was unable to pinpoint why. Zachary and I had reaffirmed and reminded one another of our love. That was clear—unequivocal. I was good. I felt complete.

Ken asked me to look inside as deeply as I was able and feel if I was ready to stop, to end the ritual. I did a brief meditation standing naked in the kitchen.

I wasn't. I wanted to talk with Zachary one more time.

We headed back to the bedroom where we had set up the altar. After taking a few deep breaths together, he said, "I'm ready." As soon as he said this, his face contorted just enough that I knew he was gone and Zachary was back.

"What about Zoe?" I asked. Zachary teared up.

"You're great with her... in fact, you are better than me... I was great; you will be better... I was great with her when she was a kid, but I was a kid... I don't do adult all that well." He chuckled. I chuckled. When we fought, I could not help but jump into the adult role and him into kid role and off we would go. I flushed with a bit of embarrassment. "You will be better for her as she gets older... Maybe 'better' is not quite right, but just more 'right' for her. We all have different things to be doing now... Zoe will be fine... "

I told him that their school community was taking good care of Zoe by honoring her grieving process;

"Yeah, I kind of get that... I don't get all the details . . ."

I asked him about where he was. "I don't quite know... I was really scared and confused at the beginning but now being here is a bit easier... My heart hurt... I missed you two... " He went on to reassure me that all was okay with him and that all would be well with Zoe and me.

*Scary and confusing? You mean it doesn't get easier once you die? What about all that white light stuff?*

I knew if he had any awareness after he was struck, he would be worried about us and that he would be afraid, but somehow I thought there would be total relief from all of that once he lost consciousness or at the latest, once he passed... Apparently with the suddenness of his passing that was not quite true.

"Its not the same as you, but my heart broke too... I did not want to go..."

"I am trying to figure out the rules..." He went on to reassure me that all was okay with him and that all would be okay with Zoe and me. "Leaving you was so hard... I didn't want to go, but I had to..."

I am sure that I grimaced. "I know you did not want me to leave... I feel so terrible about that..."

I sort of snorted. The last thing I wanted from him was to feel bad for dying. Through my tears I said, "I know... I know..." Somehow words were not coming.

"I know you hurt like never before. I know you are afraid, but, please, don't be afraid." His face took on a stern intensity when he talked about my fear.

Silent tears were running down my face. I did not know what more to say. In a moment of what I now see as sheer absurdity, I asked, "Should I sell the 34th Street house?"

He laughed and said, "Honey, I don't sell houses... you are on your own... Sell the house; it is okay... I do not sell houses... " And he laughed again.

I tried to laugh with him, but the sound came out was some sick amalgamation of a chuckle, fear, and heartbreak.

"I want to take you wherever I end up. I promise…" was all I could say. He softened, "I am not sure that it's a good idea for you. I am not sure why, but I don't think the rules allow for that. Plus, you need to do what's next for you two on your own. It'll be better for you and Zoe if you do…"

*The fucking rules.*

I knew I could not "take him with me" as much as I could not make him undead, but I was grabbing for something, anything. This encounter rekindled my longing for him.

*More letting go.*

I wanted to keep talking but knew there was nothing more to say. Ken looked strained, slightly ragged and noticeably pale. The experience was hard on his body—of that I was certain.

The time had come; I had to say goodbye to Zachary again. I did not believe I could do it.

*How can I do this? How can I face this goodbye with consciousness and clarity? Can I find the courage and grace?*

"I love you," I said. "Go. It is okay. Do what you need to do. I will figure it out."

It was true.

I always say, "I will figure it out" when I have no real idea what to do or where to go. Zachary knew this about me.

He smiled and mumbled back, "You'll figure it out. Of course, you will."

It was true; I would. "Go fly with the angels."

He told me again, "I love you. I am so glad we did what we did together. I love Zoe, and she will be fine… I am sorry, you know?"

I knew. And for this last exchange, I am grateful beyond words. When he was being tender, he would always end his thought with the inflection of a question. Until I heard this again, I had almost forgotten this about him. He faded away.

Ken returned and was not okay. He was shaky, pale, and looked more than a bit dazed. His eyes were glassy and off. I was worried about him. I could not face another loss. I could hardly believe what was happening. Ken sat on the edge of the bed, and I brought him some tea. He began to sip the tea and slowly return to himself.

I wanted to throw a tantrum and plead for Zachary's return. I was a puddle—exhausted, elated, devastated, confused, reassured, humbled, empty, full, and very, very sad.

Clearly, it was time to end the ritual. After I told Ken what had transpired, we were quiet for some time sitting at the altar. We then slowly, quietly, dismantled the altar and released the circle. The dirt and pee went to the tree, Zachary's ring went back to my everyday altar, the flame snuffed, the incense was taken outside.

Ken's color returned, and his shakiness subsided. He said that he was feeling an odd combination of exhaustion and nervous energy. We talked some, cried a bit, and were comfortably quiet for a while. I was emotionally and physically exhausted and fell into a hard deep sleep. Ken showered until the water ran cold before he was able to settle into sleep.

The next morning, I woke up feeling lucky. *Who gets to have one last conversation with their dead spouse? Who gets to feel so loved? Who gets to say, "I love you" without the usual ego filters in the way? Who gets to hear "I love you" from the dead?* Truly, I felt complete. I had said all I needed to say. That night was a gift of infinite magnitude. Given that he remained dead, I could not want anything more from him. That, too, was a gift.

At one time, I would have been highly skeptical about a story like this. But Zachary and Ken had consciously and intentionally exchanged cum and pee a number of times the year before Zachary's death. On an energetic level, their bodies were connected and familiar. I suspect that the numinous quality of these particular fluids, coupled with their intentional exchanges, set the stage for that evening. But I don't really know how. I do not understand the why. Zachary knew I needed some care and somehow pulled off something akin to a miracle to give it to me.

*Or did Ken and I pull off the miracle?*

When I struggle with my doubt or skepticism about the spirit world (which I often do), I remember that magical, life-changing night. When I struggle with doubt or skepticism about using the erotic to engage and invite magic, spirits, and the gods, I remember that night. When I feel afraid or overwhelmed by this new life I am creating; I remember that night.

*Don't be afraid.*

Intense eroticism preceded the magic/the gift/the healing of that night. Intense eroticism allowed me the most sacred gift I have ever received: communication with my Zachary.

*Game over.*

While I do not doubt that Zachary is dead, I now know that much happens after we die. "Game over" is both true and not true. *Game over. Zachary is dead. Home is no longer me, Zachary, and Zoe. Game over.* A tiny jar of ash on my altar, my wedding ring mostly buried in the ash—that is what is left of his body and of what used to be home. All of our inside jokes, sweet nothings, intimacy, co-parenting, and so forth are gone. *Finished. Game over.* The deep knowing of someone for fifteen years is done. *Irrelevant. Game over.*

What is not over is that I know "The Mystery" is alive. The mystery of the spirit world revealed itself to me. That we inhabit bodies, as opposed to being bodies, is real. This knowledge is no longer just an idea or a belief. It is concrete.

Although I have no idea what happens when we die, I know something happens that is both disquieting and comforting. The part of me that savors control wants to know more. I want to know "the rules." I want to know how it all works.

The part of me willing to enter into ritual space is comforted by knowing that in the mystery of ritual, indeed of life itself, all things can happen. What happens after we die is part of that mystery. I wish to continue to welcome the mystery of life while keeping my fear of the unknown at bay.

*Don't be afraid.*

Every day I struggle to be at peace with the mystery. Some days I get glimmers.

# CHAPTER 15

*Where you used to be, there is a hole in the world, which*
*I find myself constantly walking around in the daytime,*
*and falling into at night.*
*I miss you like hell.*

—*Edna St. Vincent Millay*

AS TIME PASSED from that fateful ritual, I became even more aware of letting go. Our history was held in the family.

I was the photographer and Zachary was the storyteller. Zachary had loved his work, his home, his husband and our child. I had been the counselor who loved my work, my husband, my home, and our child. We had created stories, adventures, and embraced our lives. A rich, textured history was held in our collective family memories.

History continued to slip away. When I recalled Zoe taking her first step, eating her first solid food, speaking her first words, being sick with cryptosporidium, beginning kindergarten, these specific memories were intact. When I could not recall a specific event or milestone my heart hurt—it still does.

There is no longer another being who can help jog my memory. There is no longer Zachary who had shared the experiences and shared the responsibility of recording those events.

In college, I learned that when I crammed for an exam high on caffeine, being high on caffeine during the exam led to better recall. State-dependent learning is the psychological term for this phenomenon. So, if I experienced Zoe's milestones with Zachary, I would remember those milestones more fully with Zachary. In his absence, the stories are cracked—the container in which they were held is broken, porous, and therefore, the stories fade. I cannot recall many of them with any real color or texture. Often the memory is so fuzzy, it is useless without him close at hand. *A non-memory.*

A memory of what is missing, as opposed to a memory of what existed; a memory not remembered is all that's left. Not having my child's story intact is another painful loss caused by, yet separate from, his death. The memories are not all there. They dispersed as Zachary's essence and ashes dispersed.

I am always aware of my cracked memories and am sad for Zoe that I can no longer be an accurate historian for her. Who knew that memories are held in the intimate bond of marriage?

In addition to letting go of shared family memories, I had to let go of home. Home is synonymous with family. When I was a part of Zachary, Zoe, and me, I was at home wherever we were—in a car, a plane, a tent, a crappy hotel or a luxury hotel, a guest in someone's home, or while in separate parts of the world. Home was my family; my family was home.

The first excruciating step in finding home again was to let go of home as I had known it. To this day, I struggle to find and create home without Zachary.

One part of letting go of my old concept of family was strictly non-metaphorical. I wanted to let go of the house in which we were living. The house on 34th was supposed to be a short stop on our path to our new beach home. Although I was not yet decided on where we would end up, whether the beach or elsewhere, the moment Zachary died, I felt no connection to the 34th Street house. With the beach home now on hold, the house on 34th was a structure that no longer fit. It had no context, it was not home, and I felt homeless. I was homeless. The 34th structure did not hold me well. It was quickly becoming a prison.

In the pursuit of creating a new life for Zoe and me, more of our history had to be released. Zachary, Zoe, and I had lived with hand-me-down garage sale furniture for years with every intention of purchasing swanky modern furniture when we moved into our newly built beach home. To stage the 34th Street house for this unexpected sale, virtually all of our ratty furniture had to go. With our furniture went more of our collective memories, our history, and our stories. I kept our bed and minimal kitchen items while our realtor filled the empty spaces with artifacts that made the house presentable. *Sellable. Alive.*

We were now living in a house furnished with make-believe furniture that we were not comfortable using, because the house had to appear as though no one lived there. The house-on-the-market feel landed Zoe and me in a structure that felt foreign and surreal.

In my pursuit of deep pleasure to create a home for Zoe and me, we had to get out of a house that was feeling like a prison. I had to let go. I had to ask Zoe to let go. Again.

Zoe had hundreds of stuffed animals, and she was tentative about giving up any of them. First, she selected a handful that she could keep out in our staged home. She did not know what to do next. She picked up her pink Winnie the Pooh and recalled her grandfather purchasing that for her on a trip to New York. Then she found another her mom had sent to her; then another that she and Zachary had picked out at a farmer's market. Her animals had stories, and those stories were meaningful to her.

Over the course of the next week or so, we touched each of her animals and dolls while she recounted their stories. She decided that she was able to let go of an animal if she could not remember how she had acquired it. I thought her idea was brilliant.

I had to trust that as I found pleasure in another home, she too would find pleasure in a new home. The house, while a prison for me, was home to her; I had to leave it.

The vast majority of Zoe's toys were put in storage; our furniture was donated or dumped, art removed, photographs put away. History was slipping, evaporating. Going to Goodwill; going to the dump; going to a friend's garage. Obscured by newspaper and bubble wrap, and locked in sealed boxes, I watched the physical evidence of our shared lives dispersing.

Our house was officially for sale. Each morning before I took Zoe to school, I had to strip our bed of our comfortably used and lived-in sheets and replace them with the realtor's crisp sheets and pillows. As I left the house, our realtor insisted we wipe down every surface to not leave a trace of life. Somehow this felt fitting to me.

Most days, our lives did not feel real to me anyway. Zachary was not living there, and Zoe and I were no longer the people we had been. The story of those nine months that our house was for sale was one of erasing our history on a daily basis.

Zoe was lucky to have two parents. Now she had one— one who couldn't remember everything that had come before. I have no idea when she first stood on her own. I do remember when she crawled for the first time. I walked in the door on December 20, 2002, and proud Daddy Zachary came to me holding Zoe. He ceremonially placed her on her belly on the living room carpet and together, we watched. I hope I never forget the huge proud grin he was wearing as Zoe clumsily took off crawling. For some reason that story is mine, not ours, so it does not feel lost. It is my story because I was observing them both as Zoe crawled; we did not witness her first crawl together. Had we been present together as Zoe became mobile, I am sure my memory would be more fuzzy. Most of the rest of Zoe's young childhood was ours, and without him here to hold memories with me, the stories are incomplete.

I miss that sense of history, of place. In the wake of Zachary's death, I had neither place nor history rooted anywhere. When he was alive, I could not feel what my life was like before I met him. I know that I had a good and full life, but I cannot really remember it; I cannot feel it.

I cannot feel what my life with Zachary felt like. I had no emotional sense of what our life, which I know was full, engaged, and fun, was like before Zoe's birth. The inability to feel prior iterations of my life was not alarming because the life I was in was far richer than the life I could no longer feel.

As the months and years go by, I continue to lose my ability to have an emotional sense of him. Or more accurately, what my life felt like with him. The thousands of photographs help me cobble together a story, a narrative, but the feeling of that life is elusive at best. And when I am aware of that absence, I hurt.

I am now creating new history and sense of place. The stories since Zachary's death are mine. They are intact. I have told Zoe my stories many times, but I know when I die, these stories will also die. I mistakenly believed that history and memory are somehow fixed. Perhaps history is fixed, but memory is not. Without shared memories, history becomes ephemeral.

During the nine months of waiting for our house to sell, Zoe and I went to many open houses trying to imagine living somewhere on our own. We began to imagine what might be next for us. Visiting condos, townhomes, apartments, small houses all offered us a peek of what could be.

Ken and Nancy came house hunting with us. Being with them allowed me more room to process what it meant for me to be shopping for a home for myself and my grieving, yet very alive, daughter. Being in a large group looking at places allowed for a more festive, excited-with-possibility energy. It worked; Zoe was excited.

"Which room will be mine, Papa? Can I have the bigger room? I have more animals and books than you." She always wanted the larger room.

At night she would often take out pencil and sketchpad to draw all of the things she might want in her new room. She concretely started to place herself in her new life.

We finally bought a newly built modern townhome in West Seattle. I knew that I no longer wanted to sleep in the bed Zachary and I had shared. While I am not a buy-it-new kind of guy, I was ready to buy myself... *Myself? Really?...* a new bed. Zoe wanted our old bed. I thought that sweet and appropriate given she had mostly slept with me in that bed since had Zachary died.

On move-in day, my new bed was a few days from being delivered. No problem—we set up Zoe's bed in her new room. She was excited to sleep in her "new" bed and go through the boxes of stuff she had not seen or touched in months. Ken, Nancy, and I checked in on her as she emptied her boxes, and agreed that she looked and felt good. She was excited and looking forward.

Ken and Nancy spent almost twelve-hours helping me set up our new home. Even with their help, optimistic excitement for the future was so hard to hold next to the devastating hole Zachary had left. *Can I set up a kitchen without Zachary?*

It made no sense.

After Ken and Nancy headed home I went upstairs to get Zoe to bed. As was our custom, I would get into bed with her, read to her, sing some songs, then rub her back as she fell asleep. Since Zachary had died, this ritual gained importance for both of us (more than half the time, I would fall asleep rubbing her back). Sharing a bed with me comforted her.

That night, after reading a couple of chapters from *The Chronicles of Narnia*, she summarily dismissed me from her room. "Good night, Papa. Are you excited to be in your new room?"

I was so happy to see her comfort and excitement. "No," I said, "I don't have a bed in my room yet, so I'm going to sleep here with you tonight. I'll sleep in my room in a couple of days."

Without a moment's hesitation, she said, "No, I want to sleep by myself tonight. We can make you a bed on the floor in your room!"

I assured her I could make my own bed and wished her good night. She quickly fell asleep. My back hurt the next morning after sleeping on the hard, cold floor, but I was elated that she was able to sleep by herself in a different room. *Life goes on and sometimes moving on feels good.*

As Zoe's birthday approached, I felt a pit in my stomach. Zachary could easily handle a dozen or more kids in any activity and make it seem not only fun but effortless. How the fuck do I create a fun birthday party for my soon to be seven-year-old—one at which neither of us ends up weeping in the corner?

I did what I was getting good at: I meditated, I brought pleasure to my gut, and asked both the gods and friends for inspiration. Then I asked Zoe what she wanted for her party. She always has good ideas and wanted a pool party. I figured I could throw money at the problem but then reality set in.

*Where to begin? How do I throw a pool party for first graders?* Ken encouraged me to breathe, and breathe again. He sat with me, or more accurately, I sat with him, as he called pools. We found one, and it was available. *Check.* Then came the details: pizza, cake, drinks, invitations, decorations, party bags. *Do we really need party bags? Yes, we do.* As I'm writing, these details seem amusingly simple. But when in shock, terrified, and feeling alone in the world, these details swamped my brain's ability to think.

Ken helped me meditate. He helped me bring pleasure to the parts that hurt—which predictability were my belly and heart. Weeks of our practice started to clear the fog in my brain and made my belly a little softer. *I can do this.*

We rented a pool for an hour and the party room for an hour. I needed help. I called upon Ken, friends, and family. Everyone was thrilled to have a specific task: pick up the cake, order and pick up the pizza... *Pepperoni? Cheese? What pizzas do parents eat at kids' parties?...* plates, cups, and sodas. *Shit. Decorations. What theme does Zoe want?*

All of the adults I asked to help took over and carried out their assignments with little-to-no input from me. They knew I would be of no help. I was just missing Zachary on this first birthday without him.

My job was to be available for Zoe's excitement while staying aware of any sadness or grief that might emerge for her as her first birthday without her dad approached. We talked a lot about the details of her party. She seemed excited in a very normal, almost seven-year-old way.

"I'm sad that Daddy will not be here for your party," I would say, to let her know it was okay to talk about our sadness along with our excitement—trying to model holding pleasure and pain simultaneously.

"I am too; he would really like the princess plates we have," was her response to me one night. He would have—he had loved all things princess.

The swimming part was easy for me to coordinate. Moms helped make sure that the kids' locker room change went smoothly. The party room, on the other hand, was another story.

The bare cinderblock walls of the party room seemed an apt reflection of my inner self. *How do I make this party not another wake?* All of the kids and parents attending were families from school. Many had not spent much time with me aside from a few minutes at drop off or pick up. As they had gotten back to their lives, Zachary's death receded from front and center of their minds. For me, I was working each day with my pain, fear, and sadness. I did not want Zoe's party to be yet another time to mourn collectively. *How can it not be?*

Ken, Nancy, and the two other adults were great. They directed grieving parents to the hallway to visit and support me and each other, and they kept the kid part of the party pretty alive and fun. Zoe knew that many of the adults were sad, but she also knew they were happy for her birthday.

I think my team of adults was successful. There are many pictures of me on the floor with kids running around with huge smiles and lots of plastic toys from their party bags. All the pictures of Zoe show her present and having fun; we both missed Daddy as well.

Who knew we have to let go of our history to create a new life? I didn't. Letting go had been put into motion by the ritual where I invited Zachary to help me let go. Although I had started the letting-go process the moment he died—and that Halloween ritual turbo-charged my ability to let go—the ripples of this letting go are still alive and well in my body and mind today.

# CHAPTER 16

*Death is not the opposite of life, but a part of it.*
—*Haruki Murakami*
*Blind Willow, Sleeping Woman; 24 Stories*

A FEW WEEKS after Zachary's death, a new normal began to emerge. Each morning, Ken and I had our time together in the Wailing Room, and then it was time for me to focus on the day-to-day realities of being a single parent.

For the first few months of school, preparations for Zoe's day were foreign to me. Making her lunch and gathering her things felt awkward, like I had two left hands. Some mornings Ken stayed with me as I went about my morning. Some mornings, he even accompanied us on our drive south.

Zachary had made the morning routine appear smooth and effortless. But for me, it was anything but. I was often overwhelmed with what seemed like a steep learning curve for something so simple. It was not simple for me because he was not there. *He remains dead.* With every sandwich made or sippy cup filled, I was reminded why I was doing these specific parenting tasks at this particular time. I was doing this to nourish my daughter, but more prominent in my mind and body was the fact that I was doing this because he is dead. *He remains dead.*

But I did not fall to pieces each morning because I prepared myself, fed myself, with delicious alive energy with Ken each morning before Zoe awoke. Our intentional morning practices moved that day's dose of the seemingly endless supply of hurt, fear, and sadness out of me enough so I could think clearly and be emotionally present. Because of our morning Tantra practice, I had more emotional and intellectual space to respond to the mundane demands of being a father.

Zoe decided that because she could no longer get ready in her dad's classroom before other kids arrived, and she no longer wanted to dress her sleepy self in the morning, she would dress in her school clothes after her nighttime shower. Then, she reasoned, she could just get up, brush her teeth, and head to the car where she could eat and drink her commuter breakfast.

A part of myself was appalled at the thought of sending Zoe to school in the clothes in which she slept, but I thought allowing her to figure out some of her own new routines was important—and it worked. She got to school dressed, not too wrinkled, hair combed, and stomach full—a monumental success in my book.

Her preferred breakfasts always included sausages and milk. I learned to keep goldfish crackers, water, and juice boxes in the car for times when Zoe was hungry or thirsty. I have scant regrets about how I treated Zachary over the years, but I was always mildly disgusted by the state of the back seat of his car. I was not shy letting him know how I felt. Food particles, crusty things, and a faintly spoiled milk odor greeted us whenever we got in his car. Now as I climbed into my car each day I greeted the same smells, stains, and crumbs. I felt a flush of shame. I had been critical of his ability to keep his car habitable for adults, and here I was with a car that was barely habitable for me.

The mornings did not become emotionally easier with each passing day, but they did become more predictable and more routine. The steps became clearer. I was emotionally present and available to my daughter. There were even the beginnings of finding pleasure in the tasks of her morning. We enjoyed listening to audio books and looked forward to our Friday afternoon ritual of stopping for pho on the way home.

When I dropped her off or picked her up, I experienced Zachary's absence profoundly. Her school and his larger-than-life presence there were inexorably linked. Now school felt oddly hollow without him. Parents and staff always made a point to say 'hi' and offer hugs, waves, and stories about Zachary. It was a rare morning where I did not leave the parking lot or the Head of School's office in tears. I felt so loved by all there, and yet, so alien. I did not belong there without him—and yet, I did.

Zoe's days at school were excruciating for her. She was in first grade in the room that was his, with the mural he had painted on the back wall; all the books he had initialed; his pet snake, Pyth; and all of the wall art she had seen each day for the last four years. It was Daddy's room.

Now it was not. Yet to her it was. And there was a new teacher in that room, teaching her. And while she was not a great teacher, her biggest flaw was that she was not Zachary.

As winter approached, it became clear that commuting to a school that was forty-five minutes from home was not sustainable. One evening while Ken and I were out to dinner, I was lamenting my commute as I pondered my gradual return to work. What I had been avoiding became clear: I either needed to bring Zoe's life a little closer to home, or I needed to move our home life closer to school. I considered both. Each had some appeal, but in the end, I knew I needed to have my people close to me to get the support I needed. I needed to stay put and I needed to set up a move for her. *Another move. Another loss. Another new beginning.*

Zoe would have to experience another loss in the service of creating her new life. She needed to leave the school she had shared with her dad. She needed to leave her community. I had to leave the loving and supportive community there as well.

**She** did not need to leave her school and community, *I* needed her to leave there. It was my need that would cause her more loss. Since Zachary's death, this was the first time I can remember placing my needs over hers. It felt crappy.

*How do I begin to look at schools? What is it I am looking for? What is best for her? For me?*

Ken reminded me, "Your body is wise, and knows what the best next step will be."

I began by researching schools. After a short amount of time, everything looked the same: the same mission statements; the same smiling kids of many colors; the same magnifying glasses, kid art, theater productions, outdoor scenes, and parent testimonials.

*Fuck me...*

Ken, who is also a parent, offered to come with me to the prospective parent open house tours. He assured me that he didn't mind—he knew that when I had to think about the next steps in Zoe's school life, I felt jumbled and confused.

*Pay attention to my body.*

When we arrived at school open houses we were treated like a couple. *Mindfuck*. He was my most intimate friend. He knew me in ways no one else did. He loved me and me him. But we were not a couple.

Well, we were a couple, just not *that* kind of couple. Teachers and administrators asked where our daughter was going to school now and why we were thinking of changing. The questions reminded me of times long ago when people assumed, with no ill intent, that I am heterosexual. I was deeply uncomfortable with their assumptions because I am not who they thought I was. In hindsight, the misperception of my being heterosexual was an easier one to remedy than explaining that Ken was not my partner, even though we functioned as a couple on school tours.

There was no simple phrase or sentence that I could construct to let people know why I was at their school looking to move my daughter, so I took a deep breath and told them as brief a story as I could. I always ended up in tears, and many who heard our story ended up in tears. School tours were not fun.

Ken was right about my body's wisdom. My body felt different in each school. While visiting a school, he would remind me to breathe deeply as I was experiencing the words of the staff, the hallways, and conversations. *Meditation.* I was not trying to figure it out. I was simply trying to experience these places and observe what emerged. I was no longer confused; I knew where Zoe and I needed her to be the next year.

She was furious. "I want to stay at my school, Dad's school!" she cried. "I'm able to walk Royal with Mr. D, and Mr. F is really nice to me when we meet! Don't do this to me!"

She was right, not only was the entire school supporting her, but her best friends from preschool were also there. Everyone knew her there in ways that people who did not know Zachary could not know her.

She cried a lot. Her sleep was more disrupted. I was heartbroken.

One day while I was filling out some paperwork for the new school, she grabbed the paper from me and threw it in the garbage. When I took it out of the garbage, she collapsed into my arms, crying.

When her crying jag was finished, I noticed that her body was still not settled. I asked her if she was angry. She was. Kids (and many adults for that matter) are not good at talking about being angry. I wasn't sure how to help her find and express her anger. So, I leaned up against the wall and invited her to punch me in the stomach. I trusted myself to tighten my stomach muscles enough that I wouldn't get hurt, and I hoped that she would find some relief in using her body to process some of her pent-up and confused feelings. I reassured her that I would be okay.

"This is an experiment. Let's see if punching me will help make you feel better."

We were ready.

She wound up her fist and punched me squarely in the balls.

I recoiled in pain and reflexively smacked her in the head. She was stunned because I have never hit her. I was stunned for the same reason. We both fell to the floor and cried while I held her—my least skillful parenting moment for sure.

She was definitely mad at me and wanted to hurt me. She did hurt me, and I completely understood.

Leaving Daddy's school was probably the hardest adjustment for Zoe. Our leaving also reminded everyone there that

Zachary was gone. Staff and families were all supportive, kind, sad, and loving as we said 'goodbye.' On the last day of school, the Head of School and the Board of Directors gathered to dedicate a garden bench—designed and created by the teachers and their kids—in Zachary's memory. This ceremony was our last at Zachary and Zoe's school to mark our collective losses.

We got into a school not far from our home. A week or two before the school year began, her teacher invited us to a meet-and-greet for new students. When her teacher asked if we had just moved into the neighborhood, it was clear she did not know about Zachary. I told her our story with Zoe by my side.

I asked Zoe if she wanted to tell her class our story on the first day of school.

She thought for a moment. "Yes, I think that would be good." Her teacher even offered to help.

Immediately after making that decision, Zoe ran around outside on the play field with a lightness that I had not seen since she heard that she was leaving her school. Not until then did I understand how vital telling one's story is for healing. Sharing this part of her life with her new classmates allowed her a way of letting in new kids who had never known Zachary.

*No, we did not just move to the neighborhood.*

On that first day of school, I realized that twenty or so kids were going to hear a story about the new kid who once had two dads and now had one, about death, sadness, and about topics many had likely not heard before. I decided to write an email to their parents introducing Zoe and telling our story.

Helping Zoe land in her new life was harder in some ways than figuring out my next steps. My steps and my desires were clear. I wanted to be the best parent I could be for Zoe, and I did not want pain, sadness, and fear to get stuck in my body.

While taking walks, napping, writing, and talking with friends offered me some solace, my erotic practices with Ken allowed me the clarity to create opportunities for us to find our way into our new lives. After Ken and I practiced Tantra in the mornings, I trusted my thinking as I navigated my next steps. When I mixed the pain of loss with the pleasure of sex, an alchemical reaction occurred, and my pain was bearable.

# CHAPTER 17

*Play is the highest form of research*
*—Albert Einstein*

ABOUT TWO YEARS into our relationship, Zachary and I were in Rome, doing what we loved to do: walking until our feet hurt, eating street food at every opportunity, drinking coffee, and watching the hot European men around us.

Being surrounded by Italian men got us talking about how fun it would be to have sex with... well... um... many, many of them. Italians are not like Americans. They have style, presence in their bodies, a physical closeness between them, and not surprisingly, they speak Italian— which makes anyone, to my ear, appealing. Rome is a very sexy city!

During one of our post-pizza walks, we started talking about how being steeped in a culture other than our own triggered our desire to have sex with these Italian hotties. Up until that point, we had not ventured outside of our relationship and were quite satisfied with our sex life. However, something about being in Rome, away from our lives got us curious. We decided to go to a sex club that night. *When in Rome...*

After making the decision we were both jittery and our stomachs were upset with anxiety and anticipation. We were messing with our boundaries and rules, consciously morphing our comfortable and quite functional container. *Nervous.* We continued to walk and talk, and by the time we were ready to head out to the club, we had created comfortable guidelines that allowed us lots of room for fun and sexy play, as well as some protection from STIs. We were going to the club to be sexual and to experience the erotic energy of lots of men (European men!) in a highly sexually charged environment. This night, on some level, was a clear and simple experiment with our container. We each trusted both our desires and our abilities to keep the encounters to just sex, yet we wondered (not without some fear) how this change would affect our relationship.

As sexually experienced as he was (more than I) Zachary had never ventured to a bathhouse for sex. He found more than enough sexual opportunities in bars, dance clubs, city streets, and parties. I, on the other hand, had always been drawn to the baths and never had erotic fun at dance clubs or bars. I've never felt comfortable flirting or cruising them.

Given my discomfort and seeming lack of skill cruising in more conventional spots, the idea of a group of men gathering for the sole purpose of sexual play was alluring. But I had a lot of shame and judgment about wanting and enjoying non-relational sex. I had strong notions of the right and wrong way to engage sexually that were conjured and reinforced by Puritanism in our culture.

Indeed, sucking a stranger's dick in a dark cubby of a club was on the wrong side of the ledger.

There were many "shoulds" regarding pleasure in my world. Pleasure was okay in my mind, but... pleasure was to be in the context of a relationship—a monogamous relationship.

Somewhere in my brain, and probably from my psychological training (even today many psychological training programs have very negative views on non-relational sex) as well, just gathering for sexual pleasure was somehow compulsive, unevolved, damaging, or shameful. Sex for sex's sake was vaguely immoral or psychologically wrong. But, as was often the case with "shoulds," it did not feel wrong; it felt decidedly and decadently delicious.

When I came out of the closet, I had what seemed like an unremarkable amount of shame to work through about being gay. My coming-out shame was of a garden variety: real, present, potent, subtle, pervasive, but not debilitating. It did not stop me from doing most things I desired as a gay man. However, my shame for wanting this more underground, naughty, in-the-dark, lust-infused, carnal experience of being gay was more palpable. I had told no one about my desire for, my experiences with, or my thoughts about non-relational sex.

My shame, however uncomfortable, held me well. Without it, I probably would have been intoxicated by the ease and naughtiness of sex club sex. Like any intoxication, remaining thoughtful, conscious, and aware while intoxicated is not easy. Given my level of psychological and spiritual development, I suspect the delicious buzz of intoxication would have had me lost in problematic behavior were it not for my shame keeping me in check.

It took time in therapy, age, and experience, and my adult sexual relationship with Zachary, to have the ego strength to engage pleasure without intoxication pulling me into unconscious repetitive sexual play.

Entering an erotically charged place with my Zachary was magical for me—and for us. We trusted one another with our hearts; we trusted one another to honor our agreements. We wanted to explore a container that allowed us deeper and more profound pleasures.

Sexually we were well-matched. Our foray to the Roman baths was not due to a lack of eroticism or intimacy in our relationship. Our newly expanded container allowed us to experience more while still honoring our erotic and emotional bond. Given our strong desire to protect our relationship container, and given that this was our first foray into playing with others, we restricted our play to touching, kissing and blow jobs. We played together in full view of one another and that not only built a ton of trust—it was also super hot.

As opposed to the baths in the United States, this bathhouse had fewer private play spaces and more group play spaces. In the showers and hot tub there was a great deal of looking and flirting from afar but little actual touching. As I mentioned earlier, Zachary had a way of drawing sex to him. Valerio, a man about Zachary's age and build, approached him as though I was invisible and nibbled on his nipple and said in a very thick accent, "nice body..." and they proceeded to start making out.

I would have thought my apparent invisibility would annoy me in some way, but I was delighted to find out that it didn't. I was grinning from ear to ear watching my handsome boyfriend play with a very sexy man. I am not a voyeur, so it was not the act of watching that made me happy; watching Zachary delight in eroticism was sexy. Valerio could not have cared less about me, but Zachary invited me in with eye contact. Through him and his intentional eye gaze, I realized that I was a part of what turned him on.

Once they parted ways, we went for a soak where we were able to debrief. Zachary made sure that I was as okay as I

seemed; I was. In a moment of uncharacteristic self awareness he acknowledged that had I been the one to get attention
first by someone who was not particularly drawn to him, he
would not have been as graceful. I laughed.

As we were quietly talking, a young couple meandered into
the tub. Partly because this was new to us, and partly because
they were speaking Italian and we were speaking English, we
didn't really acknowledge them. One of them got out of the
tub and saw my eyes widen, my jaw drop, and smile form as I
noticed the size of his cock—startling comes to mind. Zachary
and the other man in the tub started smiling, and both tried
to say something to us which we could not understand.

Quickly we changed our mode of communication to eyes,
smiles, hand gestures and blushing. We followed them into a
room where the four of us dropped our towels, piled on the
smallish bed and began groping, making out, and exploring each other with our mouths. For more than a moment I
wished we had made more flexible rules for our engagement
with others.

They wanted to fuck, and they seemed flexible about who
was doing what with whom. Without words we politely
declined and soon got to watch them fuck slowly, passion-
ately, roughly, and all with the accompaniment of our bodies
encouraging them as we saw fit. It was lovely; it was hot, and
not a word was exchanged.

I was reminded of the adage, "Constraints make good
architecture." In our foray in the Roman baths experiment,
we set up constraints for ourselves (*tapas*) before we entered
the club and what emerged was a different way for us to be
sexual (*spanda*). While I would have preferred to fuck them
silly, I appreciated how Zachary and I stayed connected while
we engaged with others. Perhaps starting off with fewer limits

would have been more fun sexually, but fewer limits may have distracted us from our main focus, which was to stay connected while playing with others.

We engaged with a few other men and after a couple of hours of playing, soaking, and talking we headed back to our hotel.

Walking alongside the Coliseum, we delighted in the details of each man: their dick sizes and shapes, what they did, what we did, their accents, the shower room, the hot tub, and on and on. We laughed. A lot. Sharing our experiences was easy. The experiences were hot; and hotter because we got to share them with one another. We found a late night pizza place, had a slice, and then continued our walk home. When we got back to the hotel, we played some more and fell fast asleep.

To this day, almost twenty years later, I remember many of the men with whom we engaged that night. The night at the baths was an intense shared erotic experience. Both the experience and the delight in the shared memories created a surprising intimacy for us. Watching Zachary unabashedly play with another allowed a window for me to know him fully; to more fully embrace him; to be a better lover for him.

That day and night in Rome was the prototype of a ritual in which we engaged when we traveled. We walked, ate, talked all day, and at night we explored the sex club scene. Afterward, we would find a place for some food, conversation, and giddy rehashing of the sexy details.

Engaging our desires with honesty, integrity, and consciousness healed my shame about liking the down and dirty of sex clubs. Engaging in this taboo with my loved one was bonding in surprising ways. Much like many of our shared pleasures (cooking, gardening, or traveling) the more we participated in them together, the more we felt in sync and at ease with each other.

Shame thrives in secrecy. Engaging in this fun activity with my partner and having it be a part of our conversations, our inside jokes, and our bedroom left no room for shame's tendrils. Our container was solid. None of what we did was secret. We never went to a club as a way of not dealing with difficult issues between us. In fact, we often used the pleasure generated by this specific brand of eroticism to help us open more deeply into what was troubling to us.

---

MY PARENTS HAD not been well enough to travel to Seattle for Zachary's funeral, but they had called from Florida every day to check on me. They wanted to comfort me when I was inconsolable. About four months after Zachary died, I wanted to see them. I believed that in some unknowable way, by experiencing my family without Zachary, I would be able to let go some more. That winter, Zoe and I went to Florida.

Life at home without Zachary was surreal. Not surprisingly, traveling to see my family as a widower was also surreal. My parents and I shared a somewhat challenging history around my coming out. I found the way out of this struggle through acceptance of them and their beliefs. The more I made space for who they were (as opposed to who I wanted them to be) the more I was able to love them.

*Freedom.* The more I loved them, the freer I was to be authentically me in their presence.

I arrived in Florida more than a bit broken but, thankfully, with scant unfinished business with my parents. Seeing them was an essential marker of Zachary's passing. I needed to see them to note Zachary's death as much as they needed to see me.

While she did not verbalize this, I knew that seeing her grandparents would be another good, albeit challenging, event. Each time we did something together that the three of us used to do together, it was notable. *Life goes on.*

We arrived at my parents' home early that morning, as was our habit—we liked to be poolside before noon. A cab drove us the hour from the airport to their house. Zoe dozed while I tried to wrap my head around being a single gay dad who was visiting my aging parents.

My mom answered the door, and we all did our customary hugs and kisses. Indeed, Zoe had grown. I did look different although none of us could describe how. Offers of food and coffee and more food. It was all perfectly familiar and utterly foreign. Zachary was nowhere to be found.

Given that we do not own a TV, Zoe was thrilled to be given the remote control. She immediately plopped herself down and went to town. To this day I am not sure if Zoe likes the pool, the food, her grandparents, or the television best when we travel to Florida.

After we were adequately fed and caffeinated, we headed to the pool. I again felt the familiar and comfortable alongside a feeling of nausea. I wanted to run away from everyone I knew. Neighbors in the building who we had gotten to know over our years of visiting, tentatively approached me with no idea what to say.

"How are you?" they asked uncomfortably.

I offered my standard response, "Given the givens, I am pretty well."

It was hard to figure out what to say. "I'm good" seemed disingenuous and gave the vibe that I didn't want to talk about it. "I am sick to my stomach and cry most days but am getting along," seemed to be way too much information.

On a funnier note, I was pulling the car around to pick up my parents when a friend of the family, who had known Zachary and me for six years, saw "me" and hopped into the car and started chatting. Suddenly he glanced my way and gasped, "I don't want to see you. I thought you were your brother," and jumped out of the car. Months later we laughed about his inelegant reaction.

My dad could not talk about death with me. When his sister (whom he adored) was clearly dying, he did not talk about it with her, even though she wanted to acknowledge her impending passing with him; and he did not speak with anyone about her death after. During our visit to Florida, he repeatedly asked me, "How are you?" his voice riddled with anxiety. As much as I knew that he wanted to be there for me, I also knew that he feared any response other than "I'm okay."

My mom, on the other hand, surprised me. While Zoe was with my dad watching TV, Mom sat with me in the kitchen. Handing me a glass of my favorite lemonade made with Florida lemons, she began, "How are you?" When I started to respond with my canned answer, she put her hand on my arm (which was not customary for her), looked me in the eye, and said, "No, really, I want to know how you are doing."

I was surprised by her openness and her invitation.

I teared up and clumsily began, "Well, it sucks. My stomach always hurts, and most days I do not know how I am going to get through." We were both quietly crying now. "But, I am okay. Really I am." I was okay. I just hurt and was scared.

"How is Zoe doing with all of this? She seems like her sweet self."

*Quiet. How do I begin to talk about Zoe?*

"I think she is doing okay, too. We seem to have struck a balance between living our lives and talking about her loss, about her dad. I don't really know how she is each day in his classroom with a teacher who is not him."

This realization was hard for my mom to digest. "I don't know how you both do it. I pray for you all the time," she said shaking her head. *Prayer.*

"Thank you, Mom, I appreciate that."

My grief did not seem to scare her. She did not need me to sugarcoat my experience, my rawness. We talked in a real way about my loss, which was a gift for both of us.

---

ZACHARY'S ABSENCE DURING the trip played prominently in my head and heart. He was not in Florida, either. *I can always add another place in which I absurdly search for him without finding him.*

The three of us had visited my folks in New York or Florida a few times a year. It was important for me to keep a real relationship with them, and once Zoe was born, foster a genuine relationship with her grandparents.

Our routine was to spend a few hours at the pool and then head out for a late lunch or an early dinner (it was Florida after all). Then my parents enjoyed Zoe's company (in the TV room, of course) so Zachary and I could go out and be grown-ups.

We would have our fun food, drink, beach, and sex places all staked out. We knew how we liked to travel, and Florida was no different. Our favorite sex club was a couple of miles from my parents' home. It was well designed, well run, and the men came to play. And play they did—hard.

Whenever we went to this club to play (and we did many of the nights we visited my folks), we engaged with men who pushed our erotic limits most delightfully. The men there were sexually adept. Variety and intensity were aplenty. Zachary and I sampled and sampled and were often blown away by our play. We experienced carnal pleasures with which we had had no previous experience.

The first time Zachary and I went there, the place was the perfect mix of hot, sexy, sleazy fun. We loved it. The men were uninhibited, talented, sexy, fuckable, and eager. They delivered whatever we desired: blow jobs, edging, light pain play, water sports, and more, more, more...

This club was our first experience with sex club men who, as a matter of course, ramped up erotic sensation to heights we had not previously experienced. The men were not tentative as they sucked our cocks; in fact, they seemed to get great pleasure from taking cock all the way down their throats. It was not so much what they did; it was the intensity with which they did it. Whatever sexual behavior we encountered that evening (and we encountered a lot) these men performed with gusto!

Late during our first evening, we stumbled upon what can only be described as a caricature of a porn star. He was tall, lean, well-proportioned, with muscles and hair in all the right places. Plus he had a dick just about the length of his thigh. He was totally hot.

Then he opened his mouth. I was appalled.

He growled out dirty talk as if reciting lines from poorly written porn. While dirty talk streamed from his mouth, his body remained inert. His farcical dirty talk quickly turned comical for Zachary and me. For years, at the most inopportune time, Zachary would break into his rendition of the character we called "Porn Star" by gravelly talking dirty. We'd both burst out laughing. Porn Star's legacy turned into one of our long-lasting quirky shared intimacies—one of our inside jokes.

Each night after we played (sexually sated but ravenous) we looked for the best burger we could find, which, sadly, often meant Denny's, where we would sit and debrief and giggle. We were grateful to each other for our ease with our newly expanded relationship container. We often noted how much harder it must be to generate all of that juicy sexual energy, only to then sleep alone. Or worse, to be at a club secretly, only to go home and pretend it had not happened. Indeed, we were both lucky and grateful.

Shortly before Zachary died, he wanted to have the experience of going solo to a bathhouse. I resisted. In fact, I hated this idea. But clearly, it was necessary for him. He went solo three times as a conscious experiment. Then he came home and told me about his experiences.

While he had a good time on his own, he discovered that his pleasure was somehow more profound when we were together.

One of the many things I had to figure out in the wake of Zachary's death was my relationship with sex as a single man, a widower, a parent, and a Tantrist. Sex in the context of my intentional healing relationship with Ken made sense to me. As Ken and I deepened our practices, I felt better and better.

With Ken, I was no holds barred; sex was pleasurable and painful in just the right combination to keep me emotionally present, alive, and wanting more. I had not had sex that was outside of the sacred healing container Ken and I created.

While the rituals I was engaging in were taboo in many circles, to me, they were as healthy and necessary as food and drink. Our rituals kept me present in my body. The day Zachary died, I made the commitment to myself that I would "simply" show up for what was true for me—I wouldn't run or hide from my experience. That turned out to be the right decision for me. I only became what I would call depressed (numb, not feeling, hopeless) a few times, and just for a few hours. My erotic practices grounded me enough to pay attention to my body, my heart, Zoe and her needs and wants, my finances, and so on. Luckily, depression was mostly a stranger. My pain and sorrow were not—they were dynamic, and I was engaged.

*But sex. Sex outside the context of a relationship? What else could it be except outside of a relationship? I was not in a relationship! Sex alone? Sex without Ken helping me with my complicated not sexy feelings? Sex without Zachary? Sex without the mutual intention to heal? Sex without someone who knew the practices and principles of Tantra? Sex without Zachary and burgers? Sex without a play partner who knows my heart is broken? Sex without words and then no one with whom to chat?* It was all so fucking scary and overwhelming.

I was in Florida, the perfect opportunity to explore sex outside of the container of Ken and me. I was scared.

*Florida. Our favorite club.* I owed it to Zachary. I knew he would want me to go. Yes, I knew what he would want, but factoring in what he would want was also completely absurd.

I kept bumping into the fact that he is dead. *What does it mean that he would "want" something for me? He is dead. What does that mean? It means he no longer exists. What he would have wanted, what he might want for me now, how he felt, how he might feel is all irrelevant. He does not exist.* That stark reality is harsh—brutal, in fact.

Aside from what Zachary would want, this was something that I wanted. *Trust desire, right?* I needed to begin figuring this shit out. I was single. I was erotically alive, wanted to remain so, and I was scared. However, I had a real desire for freedom around my sexuality. Freedom to not define myself by what was missing, but by desire, passion, experience, connectedness—by my truth. I needed to walk through this fear and see what was on the other side.

By our third day in Florida, most of my parents' neighbors and friends had seen us, and that awkward first conversation was behind us. The day appeared on the outside to be like a typical Florida day: out for morning coffee, pool time, a short nap for the grown-ups, TV for Zoe, and then out to our favorite steakhouse for dinner.

*He remains dead.*

As we were winding down for the night I decided tonight was my night to explore this familiar town on my own as a single gay man. I got Zoe ready for bed, chatted with my parents, and ventured out the house.

Shakily I arrived at the club. My arrival was a ritual and a pilgrimage, and my intention was clear. I wanted to say goodbye to Zachary (still/again) in that setting, and see what would emerge for me as a single man—a single man who looked like all of the other men there, yet who felt quite separate and other.

*How many men here feel separate and other?*

Whenever Zachary and I arrived at a new play space, our habit was to explore—get the lay of the land before engaging erotically. We needed to have a sense of the energy of the place to ground ourselves before welcoming in the energy and attention from others. The curious exploration was also a fun part of setting up our container for the evening.

I explored the familiar dark hallways, rooms, and play spaces as though I had never seen them before... *well, not really.* All was familiar, and yet all was brand new... *except it wasn't. That shared memory thing.* I had shared experiences in this club with Zachary—I did not know it as a single man; I had never known it as a single man. The club was the same but I had changed. *Changed?* I was not the me who had been there with Zachary. Death had changed me in subtle and surprising ways.

I was more solid and more fluid, more serious and carefree, more confident and more vulnerable; most importantly, I was better able to feel the obvious and subtle cruising energies. That night I needed healing and knew I would heal others by being present as I had practiced each morning with Ken. The idea felt both preposterous and completely, obviously true. The marriage of sex and healing were a part of my evolution in my post-Zachary world. I wanted nothing, needed nothing, and desired all. My foray that night to the club was another step toward my emerging new life.

This evolution was both exciting and nauseating. I wanted to be me. The same me who Zachary had known and loved. His death propelled me onto a path of radical change. How could it not? I wanted not to lose any more of me, while also freeing myself from the mire of pain. I found it funny (and knew Zachary would, too) that one of the first places I witnessed the emergence of the new me was at this particular club.

I felt like it was my first time there. My body was the same, but my heart, my eroticism, and my sense of self were dramatically altered. During this initial walkthrough, I intentionally focused my energy inward to be exquisitely aware of my body as I meandered those well-trodden hallways. I was intentionally invisible. I did not engage and did not want to engage. I felt like an awkward teenager in a new sexual environment; I wanted to throw up.

Walking through the unfamiliar/familiar halls, nooks and crannies of this adult playground, feeling shy and exposed, vulnerable and introspective, I heard his voice. Not Zachary's—who I had hoped to hear/see/feel—but Porn Star's voice. I choked up. I wanted to laugh. I wanted to cry. I wanted more than anything to grab Zachary and tell him,"Oh my God! Years later he's still here!"

There he was, the Porn Star, with the butt of a cigar hanging from his mouth, fucking a lovely young man's throat. It was a potentially sexy scene—but, no, out of that cigar-stuffed mouth came his signature brand of dirty talk, the same prattle Zachary and I heard and laughed at over five years ago. The talk was funny, repulsive, nostalgic, annoying, amusing, and, and, and...

I needed to tell Zachary I had seen Porn Star. Who else would understand how funny this was? He was a featured character in our inside-joke track. But that inside-joke track had also died. There were no more inside jokes, folks. There was no one to joke with about Porn Star.

*Game over.*

I almost ran out of the club. I missed Zachary in every cell of my body. My missing at that moment brought my months of hurt into laser-sharp focus and intensity. I lost my nerve to continue the experiment. His absence was taking over my experience, becoming my experience.

Starting to panic, I headed for the door.

It took all my attention to not bolt. *I knew what to do: breathe—breathe deeply. Breathe all the way down to your butt.* Zachary's absence was a trusted companion. I tried to fight this truth, but I had to make friends with his absence. I was being coaxed (coerced?) to make friends with his absence. *Okay, I can do this... I can do this... I can continue the experiment. Breathe. Breathe. Repeat...*

My heart rate was slowing; tightness in my chest was slowly abating. I walked around the club, engaging no one, simply breathing for a long while Finally, I could feel myself returning.

*I'm ready.*

Tentatively at first, I began to play—a blow job here and a grope/jack off there, nothing too intense. Then I connected with a thirty-something white guy who loved getting his throat fucked—he clearly loved that kind of play.

We communicated brilliantly without words. He wanted me to take him to his physical edge—and then wanted more. He understood that I take men to their erotic, emotional, and energetic edges with ease, kindness, firmness, and compassion—and he wanted it all.

This type of clear, wordless communication, the subtle "yes" and "no" cues which inform this particular genre of sexual dance, astounds and intoxicates.

Our erotic exchange looked like I was getting exactly what I wanted (complete dominance), and I was. In reality, his need to be pushed, to explore his limits, was directing my behaviors. He wanted my cock in his throat. He wanted to keep it there for as long as possible. He needed some erotic roughness at that spot.

I happily obliged. Playing rough right up to his physical and emotional limit created a high erotic charge for each of us. I stopped just before he gagged. I stopped just as he needed air...

...only to begin again. His hunger to be fed—my hunger to feed. On a much more subtle level I was entirely receptive and responsive to his needs, his body's limits, his wants, and his pleasure. We were dancing with dominance and submission—each of us leading and following.

Although our body positions had not changed, my cock never left his throat; he was fucking me: going for what he wanted, knowing I would receive pleasure. I remembered at that moment when one takes yin or yang to the extreme, the two energies transform into one another.

This physical energy exchange, this "external" marriage of dominance (yang) and submission (yin) mirrored the "internal" marriage of *yin/yang* energies in me. When there is transformation outside, there is transformation inside. *As within, so without.* Allowing these yin and yang energies to dance is at the root of Tantric practice. It is often referred to as the "inner marriage."

Heterosexual, cis-gendered Tantrists explore this same marriage of yin and yang; men (who are often yang energy dominant) erotically engage with women (who are often yin energy dominant) and create the external marriage. In our lineage of Tantra we acknowledge the now obvious fact that we all embody both yin and yang energies to varying degrees regardless of our biological genders. Yin energies are often carelessly referred to as feminine while yang energies are often carelessly referred to as masculine. Yin and yang energies are not gender based, and to make them so, loses the nuance of these energies—vis-a-vis gender, culture and biology.

Next, I ran into a sexy Cuban man lying on his belly wanting to be fucked. We started to play a bit, and then we played harder. I fucked him, hard, and he met me energetically and physically. Again, my pleasure was fueling his pleasure, which was fueling my pleasure. He wanted me to be rougher with him. While fucking him, I noticed some subtle movement of his neck and mouth; in response, I began to apply pressure to his neck and throat. His body softened, and in response, my body softened—he loved "giving up" that control.

I was gently and consciously applying pressure to his throat slightly restricting air flow; the more I did this, the more he melted into his and my pleasure. Our fucking became slow and deliberate and actually quite subtle. The energy exchange around his throat and by applying pressure to his neck became the highly charged, sexy part of the encounter. So hot was this almost choking, I decided I wanted to cum—and I knew that he wanted to cum as well.

We continued to fuck and play with his offering up his throat and neck to me. Every time I stopped, he wanted more. We brought ourselves to the edge of cumming a number of times and delightfully backed away only to ramp up the intensity again. I could have engaged this man in this way for hours. However, I needed to check in with myself, to remain aware of my experiment, and to continue collecting and integrating the data. As pleasurable as this was, I felt myself getting a little lost in the pleasure when I wanted the pleasure to fuel insight and awareness.

I was worried that I might lose sight of this deeper desire had he and I continued our intense and delightful play. For me, tonight was about much more than experiencing highly charged pleasure—as fun as that is.

As we were fucking and playing with breath and control, I allowed us both to cum. We each had rather intense orgasms. He hardly had to touch himself to cum while I was inside of him—my hands on his neck with gentle but firm pressure. I hardly moved my cock inside of him but allowed the orgasm to come from somewhere inside of me. I came while I was inside of him and stayed with him, each of us holding on, for what was more than a usual amount of time post-cumming in a sex club.

A palpable sweetness followed our orgasms.

I left his cubicle and started wandering the dark halls trying to collect data. I felt great, but... I needed something, but I did not know what. I began to feel anxious. The cruisy energy of the place felt good, yet not quite right. The sights, smells, and sounds were familiar, yet they were overwhelming and overstimulating. I needed something else. *More anxiety.* My pulse began creeping upward, and I wondered if I did too much before deliberately stopping to check in with my body. I was not quite right, and feeling a bit lost. *I am so tired of feeling lost all the time...* My chest was tightening. *Should I leave? Should I stay? Should I re-engage?* I ducked into a tiny cubicle by myself. As soon as I locked the door behind me, I knew what I needed.

*Meditation. Practice. Breathe. Sit.* I heard Ken's voice: "when I feel lost, I go back to the principles and practices of Tantra." I had started to internalize these words.

I knew I needed to meditate. I sat. I closed my eyes and breathed. Deeply. The music was thumping away. Men, out of my sight, but in my energetic awareness, were fucking and sucking away. I breathed, and slowly went inside. The energy of the place around me, music, men, sex, felt soothing and welcoming. My body was tingling with a post-sex, post-cumming buzz. That energy, coupled with the energy of the place, became part of my internal exploration.

Thankfully, I was able to settle my anxiety. I started to feel better. I reconnected with the pleasure sitting in my body.

Then I began to cry. Once again, I was surprised. Not surprised by my emotion; I expected that. I was surprised at the depth of sorrow and longing stirred up at this particular club at this particular moment. *Why am I surprised that my conscious engagement with intense sex would open me to that deep level of raw grief? Why, when I let myself open to the more subtle energies, do I feel such horrific grief? That is how this shit works!* You'd think I would have caught on by this point. Feeling this level of of emotion outside of my familiar Wailing Room in the safety and relative comfort of my home, away from the comfort of Ken's gentle presence was unnerving.

I cried hard—snot-dripping, body-shaking crying. I was relieved to have the acoustic privacy that the club's musical soundtrack provided. *Thump thump thump.* That familiar pain was dancing in my belly, rising to my heart and falling back down—all amplified and brought into laser clarity by the pleasure still moving up and down my body.

In the midst of sobbing, I began to laugh. My situation was chock full of absurdities. Zachary would have loved this particular evening of men, sex, and music, and here I was, meditating in our favorite sex club. That alone is funny—

absurdly, ironically funny. *The Scissor Sisters covering Pink Floyd's "Comfortably Numb"—surreal.* I was neither comfortable nor numb. I fucked a lot. I cried a lot. I missed my dead partner a lot. I was sad and scared again about my life. I had stirred up death by being exquisitely alive.

I sat in my makeshift sanctuary for about forty-five minutes, a long time to meditate and cry—particularly in a sex club. *Absurd. Perfect. Lonely.* I was lonely. This was the first erotic experience since Zachary's death that I had engaged in without Ken, my fellow Tantric traveler.

When engaging with Ken at home, I was alone and lonely, but I was also profoundly connected with Ken in a manner that was sacred, loving, magical, and larger-than-either-of-us. A connection grounded in spirituality. I thrive on sex rooted in spirit. I had just had a profoundly spiritual and healing experience but felt decidedly alone. As I experienced the aftermath of a night of pleasure and connection, I was connected to myself on a body/spirit plane, but not to another human being. This experience was a new and not-so-easy piece of data to integrate.

My experience of Zachary that night was like most other times since his death; he was pointedly absent. His absence was a massive presence. It still confounds me how the absence of someone can have shape, size, feel, smell, effect, and be palpable. Why was I continually surprised by looking for him only to find his absence? I never knew one could experience the absence of something so vividly. I was wrestling with my own denial of the finality of death. Death creates nothingness, yet for survivors, the living, it creates a concrete void.

That night I took the first steps toward making peace with engaging erotically as a single man. I took fewer and more tentative steps toward making peace with engaging erotically as a widower.

Looking for Zachary only to experience not finding or feeling him was brutal. *Why do I keep looking?* The aloneness of the evening was painful and continues to be although it has become far less acute. I miss the relational component of sex clubs that was only available to me with Zachary. Had he been there that night he would have loved to watch me, engage with me, engage with others, and we would have brought that heat home with us. Zachary and I were correct; our engagement with others fed our connection to each other.

During my meditation, I remember hearing a cover/remix of U2's *Where the Streets Have No Name*. I know Bono was not talking about going with one's (dead or alive) spouse to a sex club, but his words resonated. When I went there—toward pleasure, to a sex club, to fuck, to cum, I went there with him—with Zachary. It was all I could do.

I went there "with" Zachary to "find" Zachary only to "miss" Zachary, terribly—viscerally. Some might be inclined to say I fucked to distract myself and to make myself feel better. I would say that I fucked to get deeper into myself—not to distract, but to more fully and deeply experience so that I could feel more awake and alive. And that is how I left the club that evening. It was all I could do.

That night I slept fitfully. I dreamt that I was looking for him. It was one of those dreams that meandered through the night. I knew Zachary was present; we were running errands, mundane errands. Yet, I couldn't see him even though he was most certainly there. Regardless, not seeing him did not feel troubling. Next, we began exploring a strange land and met a small group of our friends with the intention of visiting a lush garden with waterfalls, music, and green beauty. I knew he would be sitting in the lotus position at the base of one of the waterfalls. I knew I would see him the moment we arrived. As we entered, I woke up.

I had definitely started dreaming about him! And my dreams had a not-subtle theme.

In another dream, I wasn't upset, but I was still looking for him. All night I was looking. Then I found him. He was meditating in a lush garden with hauntingly beautiful music enveloping him and the garden. Our eyes locked; I felt joy. We started to walk towards each other, and just as we were about to embrace, he turned 90 degrees and walked on. Neither of us was upset; it was a peaceful moment.

A couple of nights later, I found him again. We were just going about our day hanging out with Zoe, cooking, laughing, sitting at the table railing against Republicans, friends were coming and going. It was a sweet day, a sweet dream…

Every time I woke up, I had to remember. *Dead*. The sensation of waking up, and for those first few moments, not remembering… only to experience remembering is startling. Each time I was devastated. I hope that this particular flavor of devastation is one that heals with time.

# CHAPTER 18

*Things we lose have a way of coming back to us in the end, if not always in the way we expect.*

—*J.K. Rowling,*
*Harry Potter and the Order of the Phoenix.*

I MET JARED at a weekend Tantra workshop a few weeks before Zachary's death. He was handsome, sexy, and a skilled "rope top." He loves tying people up and engaging in erotic energy exchange through bondage and submission. Bondage had never sparked my fancy. While I found it visually interesting, I was not drawn to exploration. I never understood the energy exchange possible in bondage. But I enjoyed meeting Jared and watching him play and engage in his art; his passion was a pleasure.

A few days before Zachary died, Zachary, Jared, and I had dinner together. We talked about bondage, sex, life, and food. It was a low-key evening with easy, relaxed conversation. A few days later, I was touched to see Jared at Zachary's funeral. He, like many, offered to be of service in any way he could during this difficult time.

As Ken and I continued our Tantric exploration, I developed a surprising, but clear and distinct, desire to be tied up by Jared. At first I did not pay attention to this nascent desire; but the desire persisted over the course of months. *Well, shit, I guess I should trust my desire? Being tied up?* I did not know what or why or how, but I guessed that experimenting with Jared would be a powerful and important step in my process. This desire was out of character for me—I do not fancy myself submissive, or a bottom; I'm not a man who relinquishes control of my body easily.

*Trust desire.*

I trusted my desire. Trusting desires that seemed congruent with my history and self-image is easy, albeit radical; trusting this incongruent desire was much more challenging. I called Jared. Not surprisingly, he was up for participating in this experiment with Ken and me.

Since Zachary's death, I had been feeling constrained. *Tight. Uncomfortably contained. Restricted. Unable to escape.*

I could not escape the pain, the hurt, the missing, the discomfort, the fear. *The ever-present fear.* Breathing was often hard. I was not feeling much emotional or physical ease.

*Can I actually allow myself to be physically restrained? Am I really willing to do this? What will happen if I do? Why am I thinking this is remotely a good idea? If I am restrained, what will I feel like on the inside? Well, I guess I should trust desire even when it makes me more than a bit uncomfortable.*

I got clear: I wanted to allow myself to be bound, literally and metaphorically held by these two men whom I trusted a great deal. I was curious what might happen internally as I experienced (or submitted to) being physically constrained. I was open to engaging sexually once restrained, but sex was not paramount for me in this experiment.

Ken and I arrived at Jared's place. We talked about my desire, my lack of experience, my fears, and my intentions. We began by meditating together. As Jared brought out the rope, we continued to breathe together. As I undressed, we made lots of eye contact. I focused on my breath as Jared began to slowly bind me. He was careful and deliberate in a way that caught me off guard. He welcomed my nervous curiosity. He allowed me time and space to experience the texture of the rope against my skin.

We were standing face to face, eyes locked, as we breathed together. The rope felt unfamiliar, uncomfortable, yet comforting. I felt the rope in between my legs, around my torso, under my arms, and somehow connecting all of these places. At some point, he gently guided me toward a stool in the room that I had not noticed. He asked if I would be willing to be tied to the stool. Curious, I consented. *Everything is an experiment, right?*. I was breathing. It was comfortable and interesting, but not pleasurable.

In Tantric practice, there is often a dance between movement and stillness; action and inaction. We paused, breathed, checked in, talked some; and I continued to be bound.

I was frightened. Not necessarily by what was happening, but by my desire to have this happen. It was not the "me" I knew and that was unsettling. I liked the tactile feel of the rope on my body; I felt held in a comforting, yet unfamiliar way, the rope literally constraining and binding me. Jared took his time. His touch of my naked, exposed body and manipulation of the rope conveyed great care. Our conscious breathing kept us in sync and kept me calm and grounded.

When Jared finished binding me, I began to experience the energy exchange through bondage of which I've heard others speak. Jared did not do anything to me, but engaged with me to create a new (to me) and different container for my body. His work was a sweet and tender invitation to be in my body in a way that was not my habit (*tapas*).

Had he simply tied me up for his pleasure, he would not have gotten much of a charge. However, he was following me, my energy, my needs, and my pain. He was engaged with my energy while engaging his own. The outer marriage of his dominance and my submission was happening. Our engagement was not a unidirectional doing to me, but an invitation to connect and play off of one another in a mutually satisfying way. I was able and willing to submit and my relaxing into that fed his ability to take charge of me and my body.

I was immobile. Our breathing fluttered between connection and separateness. As I focused on my body, I slowly relaxed, and started crying. Surprisingly I was relieved to be not in charge of my body (spanda!). Jared, and to a much lesser extent, Ken were in charge. They were making sure I was both present and okay. Since Zachary had died, I had been solely in charge of my body. No one was physically taking care of my body. People offered food, massage, rest, and other practical help, but no one did or really could be in charge of my body.

I was, and it was exhausting.

The rope served as an external physical container, holding me in a way in which I was unfamiliar.

The now familiar pain emerged. It started in my belly and rose up to my heart and throat. The tears flowed. I was experiencing freedom (the point of Tantra) in my restraints. I did not have to hold myself together, which was such a palpable relief! This lovingly placed rope held me together physically and metaphorically. For the first time, I was not in charge of my body as I sat with my pain.

In the tight, bound container lovingly provided by both the rope and the men around me, I experienced freedom. Freedom to grieve in a new way. While painful, it was wonderful.

After a while, my thoughts began interrupting my desire to experience emotion and the subtle energies in my body. I needed something. My energy was flowing but in an uncomfortable staccato fashion. I wanted to open; to surrender more. I asked Ken to fuck me and for Jared to breathe with me. I wanted to be grounded. I wanted to get fucked while staying deeply connected to Jared and my breath, and was open to see what happened next.

My body was able to process the familiar pain in a different way. As I cried, I allowed the pain, the constriction of the rope, the pleasure of being fucked, the conscious breathing in unison to mix. My tears today were of a different quality and from a seemingly different place inside me. Relaxing my need to control my body and allowing an external scaffolding provided by the rope, allowed access to a different corner of my psychic wounds.

As we slowly wound down the eroticism, we breathed together just where we were—Ken behind me, Jared in front of me, eyes locked on mine, and me, naked and open, tied to a stool. We just breathed. Then slowly and tenderly, Jared unbound me. We sat in a circle and meditated some more. My body continued to settle and remain calm. My mind was quiet. My spirits were lifted. I felt more at ease, lighter. I was not unhappy or hurting at that moment.

*That quiet again. That delicious, elusive, quiet.*

My Tantric practices (from meditation, nutrition, and resting to getting fucked while tied to a stool) were all done with the intention of keeping energy and pain moving throughout my body. As long as pain and pleasure were moving, the pain did not get stuck.

Most often clients end up in my office because pain is stuck somewhere in their bodies and/or their psyches. When I provide a strong, loving, non-judgmental container along with information, permission, and validation, their pain begins to move. At first, it moves slowly.

When the pain finally gets un-stuck, it sucks. It hurts and is often scary, overwhelming, and confusing.

Getting tied up to achieve freedom? Who knew? I studied Tantra to gain freedom. This particular ritual, which paradoxically played with constraint, allowed me the freedom to feel, open, and heal—and it was kind of fun.

# CHAPTER 19

*Masquerading as a normal person day after day is exhausting*

*—Unknown.*

I LOVED MY wedding ring. While I do not particularly appreciate fine jewelry, it was a beautiful yet simple, wide, substantial platinum band. It anchored me in my sometimes tumultuous world. I loved playing with it using my thumb while it was on my finger, and taking it off and spinning it like a top on a hard surface. Zachary said that he hated when I took off my ring to spin it, which made me smile because I was pretty sure he really didn't hate it.

As we were planning our wedding, Zachary and I were visiting family and friends in New York when I remembered an article about the jewelry district—a block in Manhattan filled with bazaar-like stalls of jewelers selling all things gold, silver, platinum, diamond, and more.

We decided to visit West 47th Street. The jewelers were mostly Hassidic Jews quickly talking, weighing precious metals on what looked like kitchen scales, and selling their wares. The scene was overwhelming, entertaining, and romantic; akin to visiting another country where customs and language were only vaguely familiar. We visited perhaps ten of the over 5,000 vendors tucked away in the florescent-lit labyrinthine corridors on every floor of the gritty, nondescript buildings.

We settled on simple, heavy, rounded platinum bands, and were both shy and giddy as we completed the transaction. The rings were mailed to us so we wouldn't have to pay sales tax; these guys knew what they were doing. The money we saved on this purchase more than paid for our trip to New York.

On our wedding day, we exchanged rings as traditional symbols of our love and commitment to each another. They were shiny and perfect when we put them on. Over months and years of wear, the rings slowly cut a groove in the base of our ring fingers, settling into our bodies. They developed a beautiful matte patina that we both found comforting and appealing.

They were worn well, and they showed it.

Our rings were always on our fingers, but I do not remember ever really talking about them with or in front of Zoe. About three weeks after Zachary's death, I awakened Zoe for school and out of the blue, she asked, "When are you going to take off your wedding ring?"

I was shocked. I knew it had to come off—as it was slowly dawning on me that I was no longer married, but I hadn't been able to think about it.

I kept my tears at bay by breathing deeply into my belly and did all I knew to do—I told her the truth as I knew it at that moment. "I don't know when I'm going to remove my ring. I'll take it off at some point, but I don't know when."

She seemed satisfied. Then, a few minutes later, she asked, "Can I have Daddy's ring?"

I instantly lost my calm, matter-of-fact tone, and teared up. "Of course... I think that is a fine idea.".

To this day she has his ring in her "Daddy Box."

*No longer married*—again, the simple, stunningly obvious truth about death hit me like a ton of bricks. *Zachary no longer exists. I accept that, begrudgingly. He remains dead. But I'm still married, right? Well, not so much.*

The layers of letting go kept coming, shocking my system. Just as I integrated one part of what his death meant to me, another piece of the puzzle would smack me in the gut demanding I let go again. In every moment of every day, I knew he was dead. *Can I not stay married? Please?* I did not want to let go of being married to him.

*Relentless. His funeral was on the ninth anniversary of our wedding, so I must still be married.*

Somehow this crazed logic made sense. In my heart and mind, denial, confusion, and irrationality asynchronously danced as I unpacked the horror of his death.

My mind knew that my plea to stay married was ridiculous. My plea didn't just feel ridiculous, it simply was ridiculous. But I loved being married to Zachary. I slept with him almost every night for just short of fifteen years. I smelled him each day. I tasted him most days. I laughed with him, cried with him, hated him, fought with him, read with him, hurt him, healed him, touched him, missed him, thought with him, planned with him, fucked him, called him, cooked with him, comforted him, parented with him, ate with him. And laughed with him; we laughed a lot. And he did all that back to and with me. *Can't I stay married? Just for a little bit?*

The problem is that dead people do not stay married. They are problematic that way. Living people married to dead people don't do very well on any measure of wellness. As it turns out, death is not good for marriage.

A couple of months later Zoe again asked about my ring.

I had already been pondering her question for a while. I was getting close to a decision. I was going to take the ring off either on my birthday in November or on January 1st. Both dates symbolized some sort of new beginning.

While every day since Zachary died was a new beginning, the approach of those two dates invoked a good dose of trepidation. I wanted new. I wanted out of what I was feeling and experiencing now. I wanted new in my life and hated that everything was new. I was ambivalent about letting go of the old.

As my birthday approached, I couldn't think of a way to have a happy birthday. Happy and birthday together seemed impossible.

Since I was not going to have a happy birthday, I decided to do something that was decidedly unhappy; I was going to remove my ring. I knew that I wanted to remove the ring with consciousness and ritual.

I talked with Ken about this and, as was his way, he was game for whatever I desired.

We talked about my intention, taking off my wedding ring. The obvious reason to remove it was because I was not married anymore. *Still shocking.* As with any big thing I do, I tended to wonder why I was doing it, why I was doing it at that moment, and what I hoped to accomplish.

I was removing my ring to concretize that I was no longer married to Zachary and let go of another tendril of our relationship. I wanted my inside experience to match my outside experience. I was beginning to feel less married, and I wanted to use the absence of a ring to remind myself of that fact.

I wanted to use the closing of this chapter in my life to serve as a springboard to my new life. I wanted this ritual to open me to what the gods had in store for me, and to remind me to trust the forces in the universe. Opening myself as I removed my ring was my intention.

I believed my body would want to shut down and internally mourn as I removed the ring. I imagined keeping an open heart while removing it would be difficult as I symbolically ended the marriage in my heart and my head. I was afraid of shutting down.

In the days preceding my birthday, Ken and I created a ritual that held the intention of getting, being, and remaining open while I actively initiated this ending. As the day approached, I was very aware that I was wearing my ring. I had begun the process of ending. I was letting go. I loved my ring for all it represented, a symbol of our love and commitment. We loved well and had honored our commitments.

My birthday arrived. The day was lonely and sad. Some people reached out; others did not. I was listless, restless, and profoundly despairing. As the sun set and darkness overtook the gray November light, Ken and I began our ritual.

We sat for an extended meditation which I used to inhabit my body as fully as possible and brought awareness to my ring, my finger, my heart, and my belly. I missed Zachary. I began to feel lost and tight. I completed the meditation using my breath to open and relax my body from butt sphincter to crown. *Not easy. And not all that successful.*

After our meditation, I talked with Ken about my ring and what it meant to me to both have it on and to take it off. I told him the story of my ring. I recalled how Zachary had asked me to marry him in Little Italy in San Francisco eating pizza and watching the city through large windows. I told him about West 47th Street, and about our wedding ceremony at the beach.

Ken and I began to engage erotically. We had no specific plan; we simply engaged and trusted that our desires would lead us to where we needed to go. They did.

I am decidedly a top (more dominant than not). However, in the last year of Zachary's life, I wanted to learn how to be a bottom (more specifically, his bottom). I wanted to understand fucking from the bottom. I realized that my natural dominance made being primarily a top easy for me. While topping, I play with both my yang and my sexual partner's yin energies. The dance of these two energies became more and more profound and pleasurable the more I engaged my yin energies as a top.

I wanted to play with and experience my yin energy, while being fucked, as a path to my yang energies. I wanted to physically understand how I could open to insight and awareness by negotiating a completely different path to disparate pleasures. I wanted more freedom and wanted to learn to open in more than one way.

After negotiating through some baffling resistance from Zachary, he taught me how to bottom—how to get fucked. While it was pleasurable and compelling, it was not my preferred way of engaging sexually. However, there were times where being fucked was just what I needed and wanted, and I was glad to have the freedom to engage erotically in that way. It was always sexy and fun.

Tantric sex is all about opening—opening yourself physically while being fucked, opening another physically when you are fucking. Energetic openings follow physical openings. My whole-body orgasms inhabit these energetic openings. The more I am able to open while fucking or being fucked, the more open I allow my partner to be. Cum exchange is another energetic opening to deep pleasure (the inner marriage at work again).

As Ken and I began our sexual play, I knew at that moment I wanted and needed to be fucked—the desire unabashedly and unmistakably showed up. But I wanted to be in control because I wanted to use that energy somehow to assist me, in some nebulous way, in removing my ring. When the desire showed up, it was not rational or logical, but I trusted that this desire was somehow part and parcel of my desire to remove my ring. The entire ritual was a submission. I was submitting to what was real and true—I was no longer married. Yet, in some paradoxical desire game, I needed to be in control of my submission. As Ken and I played, he was on his back. I deliberately and intentionally sat on his cock.

It started to hurt—a lot. I welcomed the pain. As confusing as that was, welcoming the pain made sense. Removing the ring was going to hurt. Experiencing pain while in the erotic ritual also made sense.

I then had the desire to use poppers. Ken and I had used them together a handful of times, but they were not a large part of either of our sexual repertoires. Poppers, an inhalant, is a catch-all phrase for various alkyl nitrates that enhance sexual pleasure by relaxing smooth muscles throughout the body, including anal sphincter muscles.

I inhaled some poppers and relaxed on his cock. While deeply pleasurable, the pain was sharply present. Ken was deep inside me, the poppers enhancing my experience of what evolved into deep pleasure right along with physical pain. I began to remove my ring.

Grief hit hard; I felt nauseated. My heart hurt while I was being fucked in the most loving and conscious manner possible. The combination of sexual and emotional pleasure, coupled with my psychic and physical pain, intensified by the poppers, blew me wide open.

I was simultaneously experiencing the pleasure of being fucked and the pain of removing my ring. *All at once.* His cock energetically opened my root chakra, activating kundalini energy, and his potently alive sexual energy instantaneously moved up my spine. I was surprisingly open at my crown chakra, was profoundly alive, buzzing, awake, and unbearably sad.

As my crown chakra opened, I felt filled with life. The experience included a dynamic quiet that was similar in feel to previous quiet mind experiences Ken and I had shared. I felt full from Ken's cock inside me; I felt his cock pulsing with life and pleasure. His sexy energy was pulsing up my spine and reverberating on the top of my head. I felt filled from above (not from his cock) with something akin to liquid comfort. The comfort was opening me to the moment of pleasure, to that moment of okay-ness.

The actual removal of the ring was reminiscent of the pain I felt when closing Zachary's casket. Both actions felt unfathomable. I was in the middle of an erotic ritual to un-marry; I was removing my ring. *He is dead, and I am no longer married. How was any of this possible?* Through the sex, the poppers, and the love, removing the ring began to make some sense. It did not feel good, but I got a peek into my new ringless reality.

I tentatively removed the ring only to put it back on because I could not bear the finality. I must have tried four or five times before I was able to remove it and place it on my altar. But I did. It stayed on the altar for quite some time.

Years later, I still miss my ring and still unconsciously use my thumb to play with it only to realize it's not there. I still miss being married to Zachary. However, these feelings of loss and grief are not stuck or toxic to me. My missing of him feels bitter/sweet.

There is no way I would have planned to use poppers in a ritual. We had planned erotic play where we trusted our desire while each holding our intention. Desire, not thinking or planning, led us to poppers—and they facilitated a greater opening all over my body.

*Trust desire. Radical. Fucking radical.*

*Happy fucking birthday.*

# CHAPTER 20

*I've learned that people will forget what you said, people will forget what you did, but people will never forget how you made them feel.*

—Maya Angelou

THE FIVE-POUND NONDESCRIPT brown plastic box of Zachary's cremains sat under my bed for months. Because our house was for sale, our realtor—who was also a dear friend—advised us against keeping an altar while potential buyers were touring the house, which made sense. Where does one keep the ashes of a loved one when one's house is for sale? Yet another of the absurdities I faced while processing Zachary's death.

Zoe resisted taking down the altar we had set up the morning Zachary had died. It somehow comforted her in ways neither she nor I could articulate. I hated having her hide all the evidence that we were a family missing Daddy. I hated hiding death. Not only did we hide death and grief, but we also hid all traces of who we were. I desperately needed to be out of that house.

"Can we have an altar outside?" she asked one day.

"Of course we can."

We traipsed around the yard and found a spot that was not obvious to a casual observer.

"We can't have pictures out here because the rain will ruin them. We can't have his wallet out here for the same reason." I did not like the tone of talking about what we could not have here. "What would you like to do at the outdoor altar?" I finally asked.

She hastily arranged some larger rocks from the garden at the base of a bright red lace-leaf maple tree. Looking around some more, she went inside and found the boot that started the altar the morning he had died. We brought that outside, along with a couple of candles. Zoe seemed satisfied. It was complete for her.

A couple of days later, we were out at the altar site, and I spotted a small pot of succulents Zachary had planted. I took them and placed them next to the boot.

"Can we put them in the boot?" Zoe wondered.

"Let's try!" So we proceeded to remove the plants from the pot and placed them with dirt and some tiny rocks in the boot. The outside altar was perfect.

We hardly visited it again.

Months later, in the spring, we sold our house and were able to move into a fun apartment downtown.

After our unpacking was complete, I realized that I had the energy and desire to do something with the box of ashes that had lived under the bed for all of these months. I invited Zoe to join me in creating an altar in our new home, placing the ashes in the center.

"This is not something I want to keep forever," I explained, preparing her for the changes about to happen. "I was thinking about spreading Daddy's ashes by the beach where we used to picnic."

*How do I explain what I mean by "spreading" ashes to a seven year old?*

She had no concept of cremation, even though I did my best to explain it to her. Neither she nor I had handled or spread ashes before. There was nothing in her experience I could use to help her understand my desire to create a ritual for scattering Zachary's ashes. So I kept talking to her about it.

Zachary's family wanted an intimate family-only time to spread his ashes and I wanted to honor his family. Zachary's siblings, my siblings, nieces and nephews, and Zoe's best friend from school, Melanie, were there for the first part of the ritual.

Like most things, the intention of this ritual was to assist Zoe and me in moving in to our new life without Zachary. During these past months, new people joined my inner circle of trusted loved ones. I wanted to include them in this scattering of the ashes ritual as well. So we decided to scatter the ashes in two shifts.

We all met at the beach and talked for a while. *More memories, more stories.*

After sitting quietly, the family group walked silently about a half-mile north to our favorite clearing where a stream fed into Puget Sound, creating a gorgeous green grotto. We sat on the log where we had often enjoyed picnic lunches. Together we opened up the brown box. I was caught short when I saw the fine, gray, lumpy ash. *Ash? Is this all that's left?*

I brought Zoe over and held her while she peered into the box and plastic bag to see what was left of her dad. The sight made no sense to her and only made a slight bit more sense to me. I explained that we would each take handfuls of ash and throw or place them where we wanted. She did not want to touch them.

*I don't blame her. I don't want to touch them either.*

I took the first handful, walked to the water's edge and tossed them into the water. "Go fly with the angels," I said quietly, remembering that is what I said to "him" when I saw his wrecked body at the hospital and what I said to "him" when we said goodbye during the Halloween ritual.

Others took some ashes and quietly drifted to different parts of the clearing: some to the stream, some to the logs, some into the woods, and others right in the center of the clearing.

Soon, Zoe and Melanie approached the box, took some ashes, and started walking around. They did not know where they wanted to place them. Then, the instant I was not watching them, laughter erupted. They were running around and laughing, throwing ashes. I was initially taken aback, and then my heart cracked open, and I smiled. It was another of those moments where I felt like all was okay in the world. Zachary's kid and his kid's best friend were acting like kids. Best friends, laughing and playing and finding their way through this solemn ritual.

All our moods lifted and we started talking, laughing, and spreading bits of ashes as we desired.

When we walked back to where we began, we were met with our newly forming community—some old dear friends, and some new loved ones. Our family connected with our new community.

Zachary's family felt complete and decided to pass on the second spreading. Zoe and I led this second group of dear friends to the grotto. Instead of me starting the ritual this time, Zoe scooped her hand full of ash and encouraged Melanie to do the same. They, with lightness and with reverence, showed the rest of us how it was done.

I had many insecurities about my parenting skills and abilities that first year; but when I saw Zoe leading friends in the spreading of her dad's ashes, I was filled with pride. Pride for who she was, how she had weathered the storm, and pride for how I shepherded her through this painful, tumultuous year. I did well. She did well. We were okay and were going to be okay.

# CHAPTER 21

*Allow yourself to want things, no matter the risk of disappointment. Desire is never the mistake.*

—*unknown*

"WHERE ARE YOU going?" She looked up from her bowl of macaroni and cheese as the sitter arrived.

In my carefully practiced, trying-to-sound nonchalant voice, I answered "Meeting a friend for dinner at the new Indian restaurant down the street."

She nodded. *Quiet.* "Which friend?"

"A new friend, his name is Rob." *Nonchalant. Casual. Easy.*

"Is this a date?"

I smiled and realized that hiding this fact from her was not going to work. I looked her in the eyes. "Yes, honey, it is a date."

"Okay," and she went back to eating.

"Did you meet him on Match.com?"

*How the fuck does she know about Match.com? She's eight.*

"Yes, I did meet him on Match.com" I said, slightly embarrassed, not prepared to have this conversation on my way out the door. "He seems like a nice guy."

"How do you know about *match.com*?"

She rolled her eyes. "Everyone knows about *match.com*." She was back to moving the noodles around in her bowl. "I would like to have two dads again." I loved how she could articulate her desires to me and hope I continue to be as enamored of this skill as she approaches her teen years.

"I would like for you to have two dads again... I would like to be married again. But for now, I am going to start with going on a date." I kissed her goodbye and headed out the door.

*I was not expecting* that *conversation this evening.*

When I returned, Zoe was in bed as I had expected, and the house was quiet. The sitter told me they had fun watching a movie and going out for ice cream. I said good night. No sooner had I closed the door, Zoe bounded down the stairs.

"Did you like him?"

"Yes, I liked him," I said.

"What's his favorite color?"

"I don't know, I haven't asked him yet."

"What's his favorite animal?"

I was pleased to know this one. "His favorite animals are chimpanzees," I answered.

"Chimpanzees? Hmmmph..." She was deep in thought about this unusual favorite animal.

"Where does he live? Where does he work? Does he like dogs? Does he like cats? What's his favorite food?"

I answered her questions as best as I could, realizing that, not surprisingly, my priorities about him were different than my eight-year-old's priorities. Zoe was more relaxed.

I thanked her for waiting up for me and sent her back up to bed. As she was walking up the stairs, she stopped and looked me in the eyes and asked, "Does he like children?"

My heart ached and cracked open just a bit. "Yes, he likes children, a lot." She skipped on upstairs and promptly fell asleep.

*Of course. Does he like children?*

The next morning over breakfast I casually mentioned that I would not want to date someone who did not love children. I promised her that I would not marry anyone who did not love her and treat her well.

After our second date, Zoe was again waiting up for me. This time I had the answers to her questions. "Blue is his favorite color... He likes dogs, big dogs... and his favorite pizza is pepperoni."

She took note.

As she went up to bed, she stopped. "Can I meet him?"

"No, I don't want you to meet him until I get to know him better, and it may take months for me to get to know him well enough for you to meet him."

She did not like that answer but accepted it.

With each successive date, Zoe continued to be curious about Rob. She kept asking if she could meet him. I kept saying 'no.'

I have always trusted her desire. She wanted to meet him. My therapist-self did not want her to meet him until I knew who he was to me, which takes months or longer. *Trust desire.* I could not trust my desire and not trust hers. *Conflicting desires.* I wanted to trust her desire to meet Rob, and I wanted to trust my desire to be the best parent I could.

I called her counselor to ask her about Zoe's wish to meet the man I was dating. We talked at length. I did not want Zoe to meet a man and get attached unless I was pretty sure I wanted him to stick around. This was my first boyfriend in eighteen years. I had no idea what to do.

Her counselor reminded me, "You are modeling responsible and sane dating behavior. Most kids don't get to observe their parents dating, and if they do, it's often not responsible." *Shit. More complex than I thought.*

"What about Zoe's desire to meet him?" I asked.

She had a brilliant idea, "Have Rob come to the house to pick you up. Invite him in and introduce him to Zoe... hang around for ten or fifteen minutes before you leave. Give her a kiss and head on your date."

Rob and I decided to try this approach the following week.

When the doorbell rang, Zoe hid. Once Rob was in the kitchen, I called for Zoe. She tentatively came down.

Rob, who did not have kids of his own, brought her a gift card to the local ice cream shop, "You can use this to take your papa out for ice cream later this the week."

Zoe smiled, relaxed, and quietly said, "Thank you."

Rob and I went out on our date, and when I returned, Zoe was fast asleep. She just needed to check him out. *Trust desire. Even this eight year old's desire.*

Since Zachary's death, we've moved twice, and Zoe has changed schools twice. I dated Rob briefly, and have dated many men since. Zoe has met a few, usually in an informal group situation. The changes have ultimately been good for her and good for us as a family, but the changes have been hard on each of us in different ways.

Zoe is social and makes close friendships. She struggles to leave friends behind when she changes schools, yet she enjoys looking at homes and apartments. Moving seems really fun for her.

I, on the other hand, still greet every change in this new life with wistfulness. Zoe is heading off to one of the best middle schools in the city; we live in a lovely apartment in the heart of Seattle; we have good friends who we often see; we travel and enjoy ourselves; I have developed some appreciation for fine red wines.

Everything has changed. With each positive event, I am reminded that if Zachary were here, we would not be embarking on this new event. But if we somehow were embarking on this new event with him in some parallel universe, I know he would love our new lives as much as Zoe and I do.

One night, while having drinks with an old friend, we started talking about our kids. In passing, he said, "You know, I'm so pleased to see that Zoe is not damaged by her profound loss."

He was right.

Kids who lose parents when they are young are often irreparably damaged by their loss. By all measures, her counselor, her doctor, our friends, and I do not see signs of lasting damage.

Once in a while when she is very upset about something she will say, "I miss Daddy."

I tell her, "Yes, of course you do... I do too," and then her upset passes.

When our families get together, we always share a Zachary story or two, and the stories seem to bring us some joy mixed in with our long-lasting sadness. While his death is a strand in the weave of our small, and larger, extended families, our loss no longer defines us.

Now what defines us is my being a single gay dad, her playing soccer and running cross-country, reading thick teen vampire novels, impending puberty, dinner parties we host and attend, subscriptions to multiple theater companies, and our alive connection with each other. Woven through all that defines us now is a subtle awareness of our loss.

Zoe is independent, secure, funny, and smart. She loves solitude and time with friends. Her emotional intelligence rivals that of many adults.

Her counselor and I were talking about this just the other day. "When girls lose their fathers during their childhood they seem to have huge holes in their lives. At each milestone, graduation, marriage, jobs, homes, births, and deaths, these women often struggle."

This both made sense to me and made me feel sad for Zoe. Her counselor continued, "Zoe did lose her father but... she has you, her father, here to guide her. She lost a father, but she still has a father...I bet that will be help mitigate a lot of the holes we would normally expect with the loss of a father."

# CHAPTER 22

*New beginnings are often disguised as painful endings.*
—*Lao Tzu*

AS I APPROACH my new life, albeit slowly, I wonder what I actually learned about Tantra, consciousness, my heart, death, grief, sex, my body, and healing. At once my answer is, "Not all that much," and, "So much I cannot even begin to start." These years of mourning, reinvention, and experimentation have fundamentally changed me, my body, my relationship with pleasure, with people, with food, with Zoe, with family and friends, and on and on.

How does a fish talk about the water? It is just there. My new relationships with and in my body are just there, firmly in place, as though they have been there my whole life; which they have. My quest simply brought them to my conscious awareness.

I am clearly still me, but I look around and nothing is familiar: our house, my new kid (she's about twice the size she was when Zachary died), new furniture, new city, new friends, new car, new food, and a new bed all to myself. Most of the people in our lives now did not know Zachary. I am still puzzled as to how anyone can know Zoe or me or without having known Zachary.

Given that the relationships I had before Zachary's death have changed immensely, I must appear different both to those who have become closer to me, and to those who are no longer as close to me.

Yet, I'm still me. My strengths, quirks, and idiosyncrasies are familiar; my place in the world is not.

Death is not only transformative to the dead, but it also transforms the living who courageously mourn. On the night Zachary died, I made a commitment to myself that I would "simply" show up to my new reality, trusting the gods. This seemingly simple commitment was the hardest act of faith in my life.

At Zachary's funeral, a seasoned police detective (a dear friend of Zachary's sister, whom I had only met a few times), had come up to me, and spoke urgently and clearly into my ear. He told me—he did not suggest... he *told* me. "You don't know shit about loss—and now you will. And it will make you a better person, a better therapist...You don't know shit about grief...you will learn about grief and you will grow stronger in ways you cannot imagine..."

His tone softened, "After sitting with murderers and rapists for twenty years" he humbly discovered that he, as he put it, "didn't know shit about any of it... until, "I discovered that my daughter was being sexually abused by a relative... That is when I learned about murder and rape. And rage. And healing." He reminded me that while I had sat with many who had experienced traumatic losses, things would be different now.

Just as quickly as he found me, he disappeared into the crowd.

He was right. I am smarter in many ways, more competent, confident. I am more in my body, less anxious, more creative.

I am a better lover, therapist, and parent. I now know things—intellectually, emotionally, spiritually, erotically, intuitively—that so many do not and cannot know. I now sit with others who are in tremendous pain and hold their pain in a much more whole, healing and embodied manner. I am a member of a club that no one wants to join. I welcome others to it with as much awe and humility as I can muster.

Nothing in my life is the same, but I have created a fine new life, which is wonderful—a feat about which I am proud and also devastatingly sad. Life does go on. Given that reality, I was able to choose some of the terms on which my life went. I still struggle with some aspects of my new life and I love and embrace others.

As time passes, I can no longer feel in my body what it was like to be married to, lovers with, bed partners with, co-parents with, best friends with Zachary. I know I was all of that and more. I can tell you thousands of stories (usually prompted from a photograph as opposed to a body sensation) of our time together—funny, sweet, maddening, confusing, outrageous stories. I can be nostalgic about these times. I am who I am today because of our fifteen years together. I can still be caught short forgetting that he is not in my life in that most intimate way, but I can no longer feel the experience of him. It has drifted, appropriately I suppose, to my history, my story. I still want to be able to feel that relationship—feel him, feel me with him. I cannot, however, for the life of me figure out a way that being able to feel what is no longer here or present would serve me. I suspect it would not serve me or anyone for that matter.

*Another unexpected loss.*

Every seven years, every cell in our bodies regenerates. Over half of the billions of cells in my body have never experienced Zachary. They have only experienced his absence and my response to his absence. Soon no part of me will exist that has touched him, breathed him in, loved him.

*Life goes on.*

# APPENDIX

## Tantra

*A set of principles and practices which bring the practitioner closer to God. The point of Tantra is to gain more freedom to make conscious choices about all things—big and small—in one's life.*

There is scant written about Tantra, and almost nothing written about Tantra for gay men or lesbians. For better or for worse, there are many people who practice Tantra as they understand Tantra. Some of these practices are more or less aligned with the lineage I study, and most are not.

The point of Tantra is to gain more freedom. Freedom around our emotions, our physical bodies, our psychological make-up, our relationship to God as we know it, our erotic expression, and our relationships to others. With more freedom, we have a greater ability for making conscious choices. Practicing Tantra can free us from constraints imposed by society, culture, physicality, and even injury.

To practice Tantra well, a practitioner must be solidly in his or her body. Or, put another way, the practice of Tantra is the practice of being embodied. As one knows his body and knows it well, one can know many things about his mind, his relationships with others and sometimes, the wider world.

There are no ancient texts that list the six principles of Tantra that our lineage embraces. This is a fluid tradition that is, for the most part, passed down orally and energetically from teacher to student and has been around for thousands of years. With each generation of passing the knowledge there has been and will continue to be some evolution. What I teach is different than my teacher's teaching, but hopefully aligned with the spirit of his teachings. Over the centuries, things have been lost and others (re)invented to fit with the teacher, students, and the times. Personality and culture influence the teachings; however, Tantra has been practice out of the mainstream eye and has escaped some, but not all, cultural biases.

The six principles of Tantra have been synthesized and put to paper by my teacher and his teacher. These principles are intentionally simple. In fact, they continue to be simple as one deepens one's study; however, their effect grows profound.

## The Principles
### Everything—everything—is an experiment

Everything we do is an experiment. Each action—small or large—causes a reaction, which, when explored, teaches us something about ourselves, others, or the Universe. In Tantra, it is the deliberate analysis of the results of our actions that leads to increased consciousness. All experiments yield data that offer us the chance to gain more awareness in our lives, therefore, experiments are neither good nor bad. We just note the data—without judgment—and hopefully use the data to create the life we want.

As I live my life, I decide what types of "experiments" I want to do. What do I want to do for money? Where do I want to live? With whom do I want to partner? How do I want to parent? How do I want to be a son? How do I want to spend the next 15 minutes? Apple or PC? With whom do I want to engage erotically? And how? Sleep in or go for a run? Drink another beer? There are no right or wrong answers to these questions; the action you choose is just an experiment. Either choice you make will give you an opportunity to learn about yourself, others, and God. The data from any of these choices will always point to more questions or possible experiments, which, with practice, will increase my consciousness and consequently my freedom.

**There is healing power in experiencing pleasure. The deeper the pleasure, the deeper the healing.**

Trust desire. Trust pleasure. Pleasure and desire are our sacred, trusted, and honored guides. Engage conscious desire and pleasure as valid and perhaps necessary paths to god. The more open we are - in body, spirit, expectation, heart - the more receptive our bodies are to pleasure. Deep emotional, sexual, psychological, spiritual, physical healing requires deep pleasure.

In our Western culture many of us are deeply suspicious of desire and of pleasure; desire and pleasure are not to be trusted. Deep emotional, sexual, psychological, spiritual, physical healing requires deep pleasure along with an honoring of one's desires. Pleasure is experienced from a state of being open. Desire becomes more focused as one opens to it.

## *Tapas* and *Spanda*

The collection of behaviors that gets us up in the morning and back to bed at night are our *habits*. Judging any particular habit as good or bad often keeps these habits rigidly stuck in their repetitive grooves, thereby limiting our ability to transform, grow, and increase consciousness.

Judging habits decreases our freedom. However, when one gets curious about a habit—as opposed to judging it as good or bad—lots of data about one's relationship to this habit emerges. When a person is in an easy curious relationship with any given habit, he has more freedom about his response to that habit.

*Tapas* is a container. Much like the banks of a river hold the river and give it power (for without banks, the power of the river rapidly dwindles), *tapas* is a container that holds some combination of thoughts, feelings, relationships, or reactions in some meaningful way.

When you "apply" *tapas* to something, you construct a container to hold—without judgment—this something for the purpose of increasing your understanding of it.

*Tapas* is the act of containing a habit and *tapas* patiently holds this habit in abeyance. This container creates a quiet, patient, curious, waiting—more of a "not now, thank you" as opposed to a rigid "I must not do this"—to the desire to engage this habit. A relaxed, suspended animation, if you will.

*Spanda* is the something new and different which emerges after applying *tapas* to a given habit; it is what happens when you patiently and gently hold your habit in suspended animation.

A simple, yet uncomfortable, way *tapas* and *spanda* were taught to me was by being invited to suspend my usual habit of exhaling. I know this sounds ridiculous. When I first stopped exhaling nothing new or interesting emerged. As I continued to apply *tapas* to exhaling, anxiety set in pretty quickly, followed by panic. I am sure that had I continued to not exhale, more new things would have emerged for me, but I got the idea. In this case, anxiety and panic were the 'new things' which emerged when I applied *tapas* to my habit of exhaling.

In my therapy practice non-judgmental suspension of a habit opens doors to insight and understanding. When one suspends a particular habit in marriage, what happens? When one suspends the habit of having a beer, what happens? When one suspends their customary way of having sex, what happens? *Spanda* is not often easy and fun, but it is often interesting and when met with curiosity, can be instructive. *Spanda* is chock full of data that can be used to inform one's next experiment.

**The marriage of *yin* and *yang* energies within ourselves and between self and other opens our bodies up to God.**

*Yin* and *yang* are used to describe the seemingly opposite or polar forces (or energies), which are interconnected and interdependent in both the natural world and in our bodies. These forces are dynamic—yet it is alluring to think of them as static. As they get stronger and more defined they eventually transform into the other. These seemingly opposites only exist in relationship to one another and it is the conscious integration of these dynamic energies within ourselves that is the path to God.

Many natural dualities—e.g. darkness and sunlight, blood and chi, earth and sky, matter and consciousness, female and male, rest and movement, low and high, cold and hot—are thought of as manifestations of *yin* and *yang* (respectively). In Western cultures we tend to overly focus on and exaggerate the female and male duality as though it is most important and most definitive of our experiences. The experiences of gay men's sexuality allows us to see that there are many dualities that exist that are not gender based.

In all of us, there are energies that can be categorized as *yin* or *yang*. Through practices of conscious eroticism, meditation, diet, yoga, or psychotherapy, we get more aware of these subtly distinct energies and how they run in our bodies. With more awareness, comes more opportunity for us to integrate these energies within us opening us to God.

## *Kundalini* and consciousness energies rise up and descend the chakra system

Tantra engages subtle energies within our bodies as the tools for transformation, increased consciousness, and greater awareness. It is subtle erotic energies that open us to whole body ecstatic sex. While common sexual play is fun and interesting it is foreplay to the subtle sexual ecstasy open to all who pay attention.

Tantra is all about the subtle energy; the chakra system is the subtle or energetic body. Chakra is from the Sanskrit word for wheel, vortex, or disc and is a concept referring to wheel-like vortices which, according to traditional Indian medicine, are said to be "force centers" or whorls of energy located along our spine. These rotating vortices of subtle bioenergetic matter are considered the focal points for the reception and transmission of subtle energies. It is important for Tantrists to understand the workings of our subtle energetic body. We can access each chakra both energetically through meditation, movement or specific erotic practices and physically through movement or pressure. Energy moves between the specific chakras and it is this conscious, intentional energy flow that opens us to ecstatic sex, greater consciousness, and God.

The energies generated through Tantric practices and their movement up and down the chakra system, fuel alchemical transformations in our bodies. In Tantra, transmutation opens the practitioner to greater awareness, insight, knowledge and ultimately freedom. The transmutation can happen through the physical body and that is the heart of Ayurvedic medicine.

## As within, so without. As above, so below.

What is happening in our bodies moment to moment is a reflection of what is happening outside of our bodies. The "outside of our bodies" could be an intimate relationship, a work environment, a family dynamic, or our community. Our bodies are the containers within which we practice Tantra and are reflections of our outer world.

If my goal is to change something external to my body, I must undergo an internal transformation. And, conversely, if I want to affect a change in my internal life, I must engage with the outer world to make a change there. If internal changes, so will external. If external changes, so will internal.

This principle is most aligned with the mantra *SoHum*. Or, *I am that I am that*. Repeated as a mantra, it helps us remember our interconnectedness with all that is.

We are bigger than we think we are. We are more powerful than we remember.

# ABOUT THE AUTHOR

ED SWAYA, MA is a marriage and family counselor and Tantra teacher who is endlessly fascinated by the non-erotic overlap of these two seemingly disparate disciplines. He is often on a quest to find the best burger, the perfect cup of coffee, and transcendent mezcal cocktails.

## YOU CAN REACH HIM AT

SEXDEATHANDTANTRA@GMAIL.COM